The Change⁴

Insights into Self-Empowerment

Jim Britt ~ Jim Lutes

With

Co-authors

The Change⁴

Jim Britt ~ Jim Lutes

All Rights Reserved

Copyright 2015

The Change

10556 Combie Road, Suite 6205

Auburn, CA. 95602

The use of any part of this publication reproduced, stored in any retrieval system or transmitted in any forms or by any means, electronic or otherwise, without the prior written consent of the publisher is an infringement of copyright law.

Jim Lutes ~ Jim Britt

The Change

ISBN # 978-0-692-40453-9

Co-authors

Tom Hopkins

Hara Taicher

Leigh Adams, DTM, QS

Donna Dahl

M Marzuki Mohamed

Pamela Wigglesworth

Darcee McJannet

Julie Jones Hamilton

Amberli Hartwell

Sadie Allie

Carolyn P. Anderson

Anita Agers Brooks

Nansey Sinclaire

Kevin Allen

Julie Brain Lady Anderson

Tom Kavanaugh, MA

Liana Nicolaou Ferrier

Asha Mankowska

Anisa Hassan

Betty Russell

DEDICATION

This book is dedicated to all those seeking change

Foreword

Berny Dohrmann,
Chairman of CEO Space International

To The Readers of *The Change* Series

Jim Britt has been a mentor to *Chicken Soup* authors, and to some of the leading thought leaders on earth. Jim Britt's ground breaking work in *Letting Go*, releasing past traumas and betrayals in life to return once again to forward looking manifestation within your full powers, has been instructing at leading *Fortune* companies and to standing room only seminars all over the world. For three decades, Jim Britt has been the "trainer of the trainers," of which I am only one. Jim has been an instructor at CEO Space, the most prestigious, hard to get into faculty on the planet, where he developed millions of dollars of resources as he assisted others to develop tens of millions of dollars for their own dream making. Jim is the most "unchanged by success and wealth" man I have ever known. He is an unselfish archangel, like in his book *Rings of Truth*.

Today, Jim Britt and Jim Lutes, along with many inspiring co-authors from around the world, bring a pioneering work to the market to transform your own journey into master manifestation. Their principles are forged on coaching millions on every continent. As you read, you are exploring self-development as the world has yet to practice. In fact, Jim and Jim's publications lead to this one APEX MOMENT. Everything you have done to date in your own life, everyone you have met, every lesson you have learned, has led you to this one GREAT life opportunity… the moment of your own transformation into ever rising full potentials.

As a five time best-selling author myself, as a film maker, and with CEO Space, you can imagine how fussy I am to write a forward to publications in the self-development space. CEO Space was just ranked by *Forbes Magazine* as the leading entrepreneur firm, which hosts five annual business growth conferences serving over 140 countries. It was also named as THE MEETING in the world that YOU CANNOT AFFORD TO MISS, also by *Forbes*. The world today demands more than a reputation defender to secure your forward brand, it requires that you take responsibility for your own brand and reputation in life. This book will inspire you to do just that.

CEO Space International has supported launches for many amazing works including *Chicken Soup for the Soul, Men Are From Mars, Women Are From Venus, Rich Dad, Poor Dad, The Secret, No Matter What, Three Feet From Gold, Conversations With The King*, and now the movies *Growing Up Graceland* and *Wish Man* (for Make a Wish Foundation), *Outwitting the Devil* by Napoleon Hill and Sharon Lechter, Tony Robbins' great publications, of course Jim Britt's best-selling book *Rings of Truth,* and so many more. The totals have reached more than 2 billion eye balls! You can't play around with that Mount Everest of credibility that I guard like a bank vault!

You can therefore appreciate why I encourage 100% of our followers of all the publications named, to BUY JIM BRITT and JIM LUTES book series *The Change* as a customer recognition for your own ten best close relationships or clients. But don't just buy this book, rather I endorse that you buy 10, and you gift wrap them to acknowledge your most important top ten relationships in life, or clients in business. By doing so you will retain more clients and encourage repeat buying. You may also receive more referrals and strengthen each relationship. The laws of giving will come back to you 10 to 1. When you give freely, you will always receive a rain into your life just as you rain into the lives of those you treasure. Jim Britt, Jim Lutes, and the insightful and inspiring co-authors have given you in *The Change* series, a great opportunity… more important than pouring ice water over someone's head on YouTube as a challenge for charity! The gift that keeps on giving begins when you step up and BUY 10, knowing you have been instrumental in inspiring 10 friends to live a better life. Together we are going to reach 1 BILLION SOULS as we help Jim Britt, Jim Lutes, and their co-authors to achieve their goal to transform human consciousness in our lifetime. Like Zig Ziglar, Jim Rohn, the great Roger Anthony, and so many friends who have passed, my friend Jim Britt is now a historical event in every training, every publication, and every online work at CEO Space. If you ever have the opportunity, STOP YOUR LIFE and see JIM BRITT & JIM LUTES LIVE and you will thank me personally, I know.

Their work is powerful. You'll let go of the baggage you've been carrying around for years and learn to embrace everything that creates the future you want and deserve. As you close the pages of any of *The Change* books, you will say over and over again "THANK YOU Jim Britt and Jim Lutes for creating this work." You will gain a new life of super focus as never before and you will commence to master manifest in your own individual life as never before. *The Change* books provide tools to transform results for corporations, institutions and individuals, and once applied it will be impossible to miss your future success in life.

In my opinion, there are only the following areas to embrace for each of us:

- Spiritual oneness and balance

- Recreational balance and nature

- Relationship where *Perfection Can Be Had!* (my book)

- Career attainment of goals you, yourself reset along the way

- Parenting either directly or by embracing a child you adopt to mentor at any and every age in life

These perspectives come into alignment within a framework of Jim Britt and Jim Lutes imagination along with decades of human-potential work. My advice is this work is a "BUY 10 TO SHARE WITH FRIENDS" pledge. In fact, a billion readers is a global path that Jim Britt and Jim Lutes are going to achieve NEXT for the world common good.

Let's help in this quest, as both men unselfishly donate their only asset, their precious LIFE TIME, to elevate one life at a time to their full potential and greatness.

My final request to all those who are reading my forward is that you DO IT NOW. When you think of the good you will be doing, just ask yourself, "How long will I make them WAIT?"

I'm buying my 10 today!

Berny Dohrmann

Chairman, CEO Space International

P.S. I so approve this message for all my readers and followers worldwide. CEO Space has helped authors break the book of all records a half a dozen times, which means the only record to beat can be done with the publication you are buying 10 of now. Together we are going to set a global record with one publication. Make the PLEDGE and give the gift of personal development. DO IT TODAY!

Table of Contents

Foreword vii

Jim Britt: What Do You Say When You Talk To Yourself? 2

Jim Lutes: Financial Wealth.. 16

Tom Hopkins: Before You Can Strive For Success, You Must Define It! 26

Hara Taicher: Your Personal GPS Guide to Positive Change 36

Leigh Adams, DTM, QS: Find A Way to Move Forward 52

Donna Dahl: Determined 64

M Marzuki Mohamed: Grow Or Die! 76

Pamela Wigglesworth: Go For It! Follow Your Bliss................... 88

Darcee McJannet: Effective Work & Life ReBalance Personal & Professional Life Management... 101

Julie Jones Hamilton: The Power of Change 112

Amberli Hartwell: 9 Steps to Cloud 9 124

Sadie Allie: Behind Closed Doors 136

Carolyn P. Anderson: The Change That Changes Everything 146

Anita Agers Brooks: The Power of A Name Change 158

Nansey Sinclaire: Thank You, I Forgive You, it's All My Fault!
 172

Kevin Allen: The Watermelon Sale 184

Julie Anderson: Change Your Mind - Step Into Your Power 194

Tom Kavanaugh, MA: Breakthrough to Freedom 207

Liana Nicolaou Ferrier: Story of An Immigrant Child 220

Asha Mankowska: Manifest Your Greatness Today 230

Anisa Hassan: From 7-11 to 7 Figures 244

Betty Russell: Toxic Relationships - What Are They and What Can Be Done 258

AFTERWORD 269

Jim Britt

Jim Britt is an internationally recognized leader in the field of peak performance and personal empowerment training. He is author of 13 best-selling books including, *Cracking the Rich Code, Cracking the Life Code, Rings of Truth, The Power of Letting Go, Freedom, Unleashing Your Authentic Power, Do This. Get Rich-For Entrepreneurs, The Flaw in The Law of Attraction* and *The Law of Realization,* to name a few.

Jim has presented seminars throughout the world sharing his success principles and life enhancing realizations with thousands of audiences, totaling over 1,000,000 people from all walks of life.

Jim has served as a success counselor to over 300 corporations worldwide. He was recently named as one of the world's top 20 success coaches and presented with the best of the best award out of the top 100 contributors of all time to the direct selling industry. He also mentored/coached Anthony Robbins for his first five years in business.

Jim is more than aware of the challenges we all face in making adaptive changes for a sustainable future.

What Do You Say When You Talk To Yourself?

By Jim Britt

If I gave you a bunch of meaningless mind clutter that you'd forget in seconds would you give me 15 years of your life? You would most likely say, "Of course not! Why would I do that?"

Have you ever seen a hypnosis show where the expert hypnotizes a group of people in an instant? I have and am always amazed when I see it. I used to think it was some sort of a trick or something.

Have you ever seen a room full of people being hypnotized in a split second? The answer is, we have all seen that very thing take place, we just didn't realize because we were one of the participants, or rather, in this case, a victim.

Let me explain. You just walked into a wine bar or a cocktail lounge where everyone appeared to be having nice warm friendly conversation. Then the waiter walks behind the counter and presses a small button. A large screen lights up at the end of the room. Instantly it captures the attention and takes over the minds of almost all in the room within seconds. You observe for a moment as you see all heads staring upwards into the lighted flickering box hypnotized by what's on the screen. Oftentimes there's not even a sound, just the flickering picture.

You are at the home of a good friend having a friendly chat. You are mid-way through a conversation with your friend when someone turns on the TV. In a split second her head turned, she looked at the TV and gets lost into what's on the television and the conversation ends. I know you've had that experience. We all have.

Here's my point. It is estimated that the average adult watches around 5.5 hours of television daily. Think about it. They sit for 5.5 hours, hypnotized, staring into this box, absorbing meaningless information that they will totally forget in fifteen minutes… totally! That's around 40 hours per week. The average person spends almost one 40 hour working week every week being hypnotized with mindless clutter! But here's the thing, and before I say it let me ask you that one question again: If I gave you a pile of meaningless mind clutter that you'd forget in seconds would you give me 15 years of your life?

The answer in your head right now is "NO" yet think about this. Most television is utter meaningless mind clutter and you forget 99% of what you see and hear in 15 minutes.

How about those police action shows? This is a show where we are entertained by totally unconscious people stealing, committing crime and then getting caught. Same show, different characters week after week. We even record them so that we don't miss an episode because we are watching another meaningless police drama on another channel.

Chefs and Cooks. This is a good one! These guys are put on TV as almost divine like beings. They can swear, humiliate and treat other people like low-life morons and then insult us by pretending to make a pile of mashed potatoes look like art, and you the viewer believe them, and you haven't even been given a chance to taste their preparation!

Need I go on? My point is that people are actually willing to surrender 15 years of their life on average to meaningless nothing... to total brain destroying crap.

I'm not saying that you shouldn't watch TV and that there aren't some entertaining shows. I'm just saying...

Television should really be called Hypnotic-Vision, because it's stealing your life... forty hours a week for the average person. What could you do with an extra forty hours each week? Even an hour less each day of TV watching would give you nine 40 hour weeks of vacation each year. What could you do with nine 40 hour weeks every year? You could use it to increase productivity, start a part time business, earn more, enjoy your life more, relax, exercise or spend quality time with the family.

Look at the average American. 67% are overweight 15 pounds or more and just a little exercise would take care of the problem. Would you be overweight if you exercised one hour each day? I know, you don't have time to exercise. ;-)

But the average person spends 5.5 hours a day sitting on a giant carbohydrate (sofa) being hypnotized by commercials into buying stuff that will make them fatter. Funny, uh? Not really.

Here's my point. Once switched on, you almost instantly go into a state of inactivity and hypnosis. A chemical reaction is taking place in your brain. Your brain not being able to deal with the flickering from the screen fast enough so this puts the brain into a state of suspension...hypnosis... and receptivity.

This state of suspension creates space. The space then can be filled. Filled with what? Filled with meaningless "stuff" from those that want you to buy into more meaningless stuff.

This is why advertisers pay outrageous prices for peak time TV advertising. Think about it. 30 million people in a state of hypnosis. You, the viewer has been inactive, in a state of suspension, hypnosis for the past 30 minutes watching some show about nothing in particular.

This is the peak time to fill the empty space in your mind, or "mind gaps" with their 'buy me' or 'do this' or 'support this' message. And it works! It really works. Hypnotic-Vision is how, and you are the victim.

And you know what? When people are in that zone they can't switch it off. They play, fumble and even fight over the remote despite there being nothing of any real value on TV. Unbelievable when you think about it.

Based on statistics the most favorite pastime in the world today is watching TV. And think about it… PAST TIME… that's exactly what TV does. It passes time. It makes your time go by faster. Then one day you look back on your life you start to think about all the things you should have, could have done or never did. When asked why, the answer is most often the same… "I didn't have time." Really!

Let's now move away from the hypnotic spell of watching TV into the #1 time waster. That's right. There is a bigger time waster than TV. What do you think that is? It's living in the past or future. It's bringing your past experiences into the present and re-experiencing them over and over again. Or it's living in the future with the anticipation of the past happening again tomorrow, next week, next month. How much time do you spend living in the past and future, hypnotized by what has already happened.

New studies have found that people tidy up more thoroughly when there's a faint tang of cleaning liquid in the air; they become more competitive if there's a briefcase or computer in sight, or more cooperative if they glimpse words like "dependable" and "support," all without being aware of the change, or what past programming prompted it. We all walk around to one degree or another in a constant state of hypnosis, and we don't even know it.

This demonstrates how everyday sights, smells and sounds can selectively cause depression, anxiety, or inspire and motivate.

Goals, whether to eat, mate, have a cup of coffee or take action on a project, are like software programs that can only be run one at a time, and the unconscious is perfectly capable of running the program it chooses if we don't know how to control it and choose the one we want to run.

The give and take between these unconscious choices and our rational, conscious objectives can help explain some of the more mystifying realities of behavior, like how we can be happy one moment and sad the next.

You decide to do a certain thing, and in an unconscious instant, your subconscious provides you with supporting evidence, right or wrong, on what action to take next. For example, you decide to start a new business but you have failed at business in the past. Instantly when you decide, your subconscious provides you with supporting data "you failed before," so you let the fear of failing take over deciding not to move forward. And all this happens unconsciously.

My objective is to help you to see more clearly your own subconscious programming, your own state of hypnosis, and more importantly how to change the programs that no longer serve your best interest.

The good news! All TVs are built with an off switch. Just press it and it'll add 15 years to your life! Wow! Think about that! We are also built, just like a computer, with a delete button and our aim should be to learn how to push it.

The first step is to start to think more consciously, to consider all the ways we "hypnotize" ourselves into thinking and acting incorrectly, and to create for ourselves a more sane, stress-free life filled with happiness and abundance.

There are actually lots of hypnosis techniques that you can learn and apply on yourself to gain more control of your mind and your life. It's called self-hypnosis. It's becoming your own mind-manager.

How would you rate your own performance up until now? Are you achieving the results you want with the effort you are expending? Does it feel like you are hitting your head against a brick wall? It's impossible to make improvements until you know what needs to change and even more importantly how to change it. And it's impossible to change if you don't do something in a different way.

The problem is that people most often go with the obvious because we have been hypnotized to do so. We rely on the same thinking, habits and behaviors we've used in the past, productive or not, because it's what we know. It's our programming. We resist new approaches because they make us feel more at risk… more uncomfortable. But if you want change there may be some discomfort involved.

This doesn't mean that some of your past programming can't be useful. Some of it certainly is. A good example is driving your car. It's good to have the programming so you don't have to re-learn to drive every time you get behind the wheel.

The simple fact is, your subconscious programs collectively have brought you where you are today. Good or bad, successful or not, happy or not, healthy or not, you have been hypnotized to be who you are, and once you realize this fact and understand it, only then can you make any significant changes.

Do you know that even ink on paper can hypnotize you? That's right... ink! When's the last time you saw the headline of a newspaper and said to yourself, "I better read this story to see what's going on?" The headline reads, *Swine Flu Kills 187 People in Mexico and It's Heading for the US! Millions Died in the Early 1900's From the Same Strain!* What do you think? "Oh my gosh! I better read this and find out more. How do I protect my family? People are dying everywhere. Could I be the next victim?" Your mind starts to see dead bodies being hauled away in carts thrown into mass graves... or something to that effect! Like it or not, you have just been hypnotized.

Or you see those ads on TV advertising the "cold and flu season." Really? There is now a 5th season? But we buy into it and off we go to the doc to get a flu shot.

When it comes to subconscious programming, what you pay attention to grows in strength. Start to notice what you say when you talk to yourself.

Start to make positive suggestions to yourself when something negative arises from a past program. Keep your suggestions uplifting and never use suggestions like, "I'm going to learn to mountain climb no matter how scared I am." This will only make you even more scared. So cleanse out all negative words when you begin to formulate your suggestions and substitute them with uplifting words like, "I really look forward to mountain climbing and having the feeling of freedom when I reach the top."

The suggestions you formulate must be easy to remember. Let's say you want to communicate better with others, then for example, you can make a suggestion like, "I communicate clearly and with ease." Use these three steps to start reprogramming your subconscious.

Suggestion: "I only eat healthy foods that help me to stay thin."

Reasons why: Look better, healthier, live longer, higher self-esteem.

Feeling: Self-confidence, joy, excited, energetic.

Again, suggestions should always be of a positive nature. What I am talking about are "Spoken commands" or "Self-hypnosis suggestions" made on purpose and designed to change some aspect of our life. The real problem is that most of us spend a great deal of time and energy making these suggestions unconsciously without a lot of thought about how it is going to affect our life.

We've all done it. "I'm so stupid." "I am broke." "I'm such a loser." "Why does this always happen to me?" These are commands that create or support existing programs. We may think we are doing them in fun, but they are commands to the subconscious just the same. And the subconscious is totally impartial. It will accept any command you give it as truth.

Here's the way our minds work! At birth our brains are like empty computers waiting to be fed information. As we age, our parents, teachers, role models, peers and surroundings act as our programmers. They supply us with the knowledge which we channel through our conscious mind into the subconscious (our hard drive if you will). The subconscious mind is the biggest hard drive ever developed - it stores *everything* we come in contact with and as you probably know from experience, by no means is all of this information of a positive nature. In fact a lot of it is downright destructive.

All that we have experienced through our senses… heard, touched, seen, etc., are stored in the recesses of our minds… in our subconscious. Just like a computer hard drive, the subconscious mind holds on to this information until we need to recall it or until it is deleted. For example, when you were young your curiosity led you to investigate your surroundings. When you approached a situation that was dangerous such as fire, your parents or guardians would most likely have told you that you would get hurt if you got too near the fire. Perhaps you may even recall an incident when you burned your hand. You then associate the pain with the fire and the next time you are close to fire you remember the pain stored in your subconscious and you know that you should maintain your distance.

This is the mechanism used by your brain to learn. It is also the same method employed by the mind in *every* situation. The subconscious mind has a tendency to emulate what it experiences. This is why so many people find themselves in similar relationships and situations that they saw their parents experiencing while they were growing up. And oftentimes they find themselves repeating the pattern over and over and they have no clue why.

Think of a time when you gave yourself praise. What words did you use? Do you use the same words that your parents or peers used when they were praising you?

What I'm saying is to watch your internal dialogue, what you say to yourself. Learn to examine it closely. Start to notice how you think. Your thoughts are the way that you talk to yourself. It takes diligence to change the way you think. When you notice yourself thinking a negative thought, stop yourself and choose to think the opposite. I'm not talking about "Positive thinking," that's just glossing over reality with something fake. I'm talking about "Correct thinking" that leads to correct action. It's literally letting go of a negative and creating a positive that leads you where you want to go. When you recognize and let go, you neutralize the negative pattern. You have just reversed the negative thinking in that moment… and remember you only have this moment. No other time exists!

Letting go doesn't have to be difficult. As soon as you *recognize* a negative pattern, thought, emotion or action, the letting go process is put into action. If you catch yourself thinking anything that is not supporting how you want your life to be, stop, let go of the resistance and think how you would like it to be.

Here's the way the subconscious programs work. Within your brain there are tiny pathways called "Dendrites." They are like memory channels that look like tree roots. Each time you think a new thought, you create a new memory channel, or root. But here's the important part. Each time you re-think an old thought pattern, you strengthen the original memory channel, which strengthens the root… and with that you strengthen its hold on you, good or bad. Each time you repeat the positive statement or pattern you strengthen that message in your sub-conscious mind.

Let's try a session: Think of a suggestion you want to impress upon your subconscious.

Get comfortable and focus your attention on a point slightly above your eye level.

Take a few deep breaths while you repeat the word "relax" to yourself.

When you breathe out imagine that you're getting rid of all the stressful energy that has caused all your troubles. When you breathe in, imagine that you are taking in positive energy that replaces the old.

Now, close your eyes and focus on a few sounds (3 to 5) that you can hear, like water running in the pipeline, the wind that blows outside, the rain tapping on the roof, etc. Also be aware of what you feel for the moment like the temperature of your skin, the weight of your body against the chair or bed, the temperature in the room, etc.

Now, start a descent into your subconscious mind by imagining that you are walking down a ten step spiral staircase to a beautiful garden that awaits at the bottom of the stairs.

For each step you take, imagine having to pass layers of clouds. With each step, feel yourself becoming more and more relaxed. All your worries are gradually leaving you as you descend down the stairs. As you take the last step, you put your foot on green grass which has a glow on it from the rays of the sun.

You are now totally relaxed and ready to start the repetition of your suggestions to your subconscious mind. Repeat each suggestion three times with a short break in between.

You're now finished with your suggestions as you slowly climb back up to the top of the staircase.

Your self-hypnotic session is now over and you are back in your ordinary state of mind. Make this a regular daily practice and you'll begin to experience some remarkable results.

Remember, everything is impossible unless you say it's not. Think about what I just said, "unless YOU say it's not." Well, what if YOU said it is possible, then what! What do you think would happen? Here's a question posed to my seminar participants. "How many of you believe you can say and think yourself to be sick?" Almost everyone says, "Yes." Your body and mind will follow your instructions to the T. If you can think yourself depressed, anxious, angry, you can also think yourself sick. So if you can think yourself to be sick, or depressed, angry or whatever, then can you think yourself to be better? Can you think yourself successful? Can you think yourself thin? Can you think yourself a non-smoker? Can you think yourself wealthy?

What happens when a millionaire loses all their money? They generally get it back, plus more, and in less time than the first time they made it! Why is that? They have conditioned themselves to think by millionaire standards, with a millionaire mindset. They don't lower their beliefs or standards under any circumstances, even if they are broke.

What are the standards you have set for yourself? What standards are you willing to set for yourself in order to get what you want out of life? Remember, even small changes can lead to big results. Small changes can and will lead to more small changes, until one day big changes have taken place.

To find out more about Jim's work:

www.JimBritt.com

http://PowerOfLettingGo.com

http://CrackingTheRichCode.com

http://FaceBook.com/JimBrittOnline

http://JourneyBeginsNow.com

To book Jim as a keynote for your special event contact Support@JimBritt.com

Jim Lutes

Having taught his branded form of human performance since the early 1990s, Mr. Lutes has accelerated top level entrepreneurs throughout his career by conducting trainings on personal growth and subconscious programming into worldwide markets.

During this time Jim took his skills regarding the human mind, and combining it with trainings on influence, persuasion and communication strategies, he launched Lutes International in the early 1990s. Based in San Diego California, Jim has taught seminars for corporations, sales forces, individuals and athletes. Having appeared on television, radio and worldwide stages, Jim's style, knowledge and effectiveness provide profound results.

"Jim Lutes possesses a unique ability to create performance change in an individual in a fraction of the time it takes his competitors." The core of humans decisions are based on the programs we acquire, reinforce and grow. Combining Jim's various trainings, individuals can reach new levels of achievement and fulfillment in all areas of life. The results are at times nothing short of astonishing.

"My goal is to take that embryonic greatness that exists inside every person in America, foster it, empower it, and then hand them personal strategies based on solid principles that allow them to take that new attitude and apply it to creating a life by design."

Financial Wealth

By Jim Lutes

Quite possibly trumping the importance of good health and great relationships is the value we have placed on money in current society. Money is not only truly dominating in the collective psyche, it is also an incredibly loaded subject for many. Indeed, the topic of money can fill its own book (and it has)! For our purposes, let's investigate how to apply strategies and techniques to help you program your subconscious mind to accept that the world is abundant. This means pinpointing and working to overcome all limiting beliefs around money that you might have.

The world we live in is a truly an abundant world. The universe out of which we were created continues to create and expand, and part of this natural expansion is sheer abundance. This is not a pipe dream or another Pollyanna-style belief. This is the truth. Don't believe me? Then tell me how many drops there are in the ocean. Tell me how many grains of sand there are on the beach. If that's too expansive, look closely at a tree sometime and observe how it grows taller, leaves constantly form and die, form and die. The tree flowers, bears fruit, sleeps all winter, flowers, bears fruit… you get the picture. If this still isn't enough, consider the trillions of dollars that actually are in existence in the world. It is not for a lack of dollars that there is injustice, suffering, or people who lack. That is about distribution. And we cannot justify lack by looking at how we distribute it. I encourage you to recognize the world as truly abundant and expansive. I encourage you to start looking for abundance in your daily life. More things happen in your favor each morning before you even step out of bed! Look around your home, in your fridge, look in the basement, at boxes of things you don't need that just sit there. Once you decide to look for evidence of abundance in the world, it is incredibly easy to find. What you experience when you fail to see abundance is lack and fear of scarcity. Just because you feel lack, or only choose to see what is lacking, is not an argument for the lack of abundance in the world. For it is how you think that affects your perception. If you choose to hold thoughts of lack, you will only see that which is lacking. This is why I am going to suggest that you start to cultivate thoughts of abundance.

Of course, by now you may have expected I might say that. I say it because it is what I know to be true. When we keep ourselves in a mindset of scarcity or lack, we do not receive the true flow of abundance into our lives. Money, ultimately, is an exchange, an energetic exchange using a modality that has been agreed upon - namely, paper currency. Money needs to be in circulation at all times for any economy to thrive, just like your blood needs to stay circulating in your body for you to stay alive. Money also needs to circulate in order to feed your own economy. When you notice in your life that you are hoarding your money, chances are good that more money is also not flowing towards you. Moving from a mindset of scarcity into the mindset of abundance is one of the single most important steps you can take when deciding to shift your consciousness around money. Seeing that money is an energy that needs to stay in flow and circulate, just like the blood in our bodies needs to circulate, is essential for anyone who is serious about welcoming more money into their lives. Understand the need to stay in this flow.

So, adopt an abundance mindset. But let me back up first. For most of us, we have deep-rooted beliefs, beliefs from our parents and their parents and their parents even, that were planted into our subconscious minds from a very early age. For any of you who had parents or grandparents who lived through the Great Depression, you in particular may have taken in some strong beliefs of lack and scarcity when it comes to money. You might have heard, "We can't afford (this or that)" every day as a child, or witnessed your parents holding their heads in their hands as they contemplated the bills, worried expressions on their faces. Even people who managed to become wealthy as adults often hoard their wealth because of fears of scarcity they never cleared from their subconscious mind. It's important to note that although you can generate wealth without clearing these beliefs, you won't necessarily keep it. Or you will only generate as much as you believe you can have. Generally, people who are wealthy and hoard their wealth are operating from a fear of lack and scarcity mindset. You may think the family with 'old money' are wealthy, but if they have hoarded all their 'old money' you can guarantee no new flow of money has been coming to them. Despite what you may perceive, millionaires don't always remain millionaires for life. Things are never what they seem. Putting some effort into clearing your limiting beliefs around money is essential and it is best done prior to setting to work adopting the abundance mindset.

Common limiting beliefs around money include, "I don't deserve to be rich," or "no one in our family is rich," or "money doesn't grow on trees." There are also beliefs around how to get money, with one of the deepest entrenched beliefs being that of - go to college or university to learn a skill, go to work for someone else, buy a house, put money into a 401K, retire. For many, they simply do not believe that wealth can come to them any other way. While sure, it may be the most common way, by no means is this the only way. It is an incredibly limiting way to look at how you might earn money in the world. I know for myself, I knew as a young man that was not the route I wanted to take. My father and brother, both university-educated and successful, thought I was foolish, but now I have surpassed both of them in annual income, by being an entrepreneur. If I had stayed in the belief that I could only make money following that formula, I certainly would not be where I am today, running two successful companies, and having sold two.

To clear limiting beliefs, you'll need to access your subconscious mind. While you are doing this, at the same time you can begin to emotionalize your belief that you are wealthy by picking the number of dollars you really want, and I mean the amount of money that would truly make you comfortable right now in your life, and visualizing that amount. Add the emotion of what you will feel when you have that amount, and really try to stay in that emotion, especially when paying your bills or doing anything related to your finances at any time of day.

You don't necessarily have to clear your limiting beliefs to start adopting an abundance mindset, although it helps greatly to at least know what your limiting beliefs are. Moving out of a mindset of lack and into one where you truly know and feel the abundance that is all around you won't happen overnight. In fact, it might be worth teaming up with others who want to shift into this mindset, especially at the beginning, because the scarcity paradigm is so incredibly insidious. It is common and everywhere. Think about your friends and family - can you think of a person who truly lives in abundance daily? Be clear - living in an abundance mindset doesn't mean the person is super-rich, necessarily. But a person living in an abundance mindset comes from a place of knowing their needs are met. This person knows that they have the skill, talent, and resilience required to achieve their money goals. This person also is fully aware that they have Universal Power backing them up when they take action. A person in abundance mindset is acutely aware that there is more than enough of everything in the world - water, food, land, space, air, money. A person in abundance mindset is not afraid of the competition, but rather welcomes the competition and knows there is plenty for all. A person in abundance mindset is not afraid to give and gives freely, knowing full well that the more they give, the more they receive. (As an aside, this statement, really an old adage, is entirely true. For anyone who doubts me on this, I highly recommend you embark on giving one thing daily for twenty-one days, and pay close attention to what you receive. I assure you, this experiment will blow your scarcity mindset out of the water, and fast!)

To be in abundance mindset is to be in faith. To be in faith means that you know, really know, throughout every plane of existence and right to your very core, that you have access to the Universal Power that your subconscious mind connects you to. You also have full knowledge and understanding of the Law of Attraction, the most commonly talked about concept when it comes to shifting money consciousness. When you move beyond just using the Law of Attraction and use the techniques you are reading, then you are truly employing powerful means to help you generate the wealth you desire.

There are two other essentials, however, to generating wealth. Along with clearing limiting beliefs and adopting an abundance mindset, it is important to consider your work as how you serve others, and to always maintain a feeling of gratitude.

Your work is your service to the world. If you don't like your work, you may want to investigate what it is that you do like, what your skills and talents are, and how you can help people. When we reframe our 'work' to become about how we can help others, we are able to derive more meaning from what we do. I have heard that the more we serve others, the more money shows up in our lives. The money shows up in proportion to the service we provide. So if you are not earning a lot of money, it's possible you are not serving enough people. If money is a tool we use as an exchange for value given, then it follows that you must give service, and service with value, to another in order to generate the income you desire. Financial wealth is created through using your work to provide a valuable service to others, and the more people you serve and bring value to, the wealthier you will become. Why do you think someone like Bill Gates is so wealthy? How much value did he bring into your life just by creating Microsoft? How much value did he bring to millions of people, for that matter? This correlates directly with the billions he has amassed in money thanks to his ingenuity. Bill Gates saw a problem that needed to be solved, and he solved it for millions of people. This is why it is faster, often, to increase your wealth by being in sales or being an entrepreneur, as both afford more opportunities to be providing your unique service and value to people, versus jobs like being a doctor. Being a doctor is hugely important in the fabric of society, don't get me wrong, but there is a limit on just how many patients a doctor can see in a day.

This may seem like a limiting conversation and it's possible that for some of you reading this, that you just do not see the value inherent in your jobs. However, be aware, every job is a service to humanity. When it comes to creating more wealth in your life, even if you are working a minimum-wage job as you read this, it is entirely possible for you to achieve the wealth you want if you get out of your limiting beliefs, adopt an abundance mindset, and see the value in who you are and what you do. We should not be chasing money for money's sake, remember. Finding your way to true wealth will look different for every individual. Finding your way to *sustaining* true wealth involves doing the work.

Be of service, and cultivate a feeling of gratitude. Gratitude goes hand-in-hand with living in an abundance mindset. You don't have to wait to be grateful. Start feeling grateful today, right now. Be grateful for absolutely everything you have in your life, everything, and tune into your gratitude at least once daily. An incredibly common practice around gratitude that everyone from Oprah to any random coach on the internet has suggested, is the practice of keeping a gratitude journal. Well, why do you think they suggest it? Because it works! It doesn't have to be a gratitude journal, per se, that you keep, but cultivating and maintaining a feeling of gratitude, coupled with unwavering belief in the abundance of the universe, truly does serve to keep you in the flow of wealth accumulation.

Remember throughout all of this that your subconscious mind responds to your conscious thoughts, particularly repeating thoughts, and does not distinguish the negatives. Therefore, if you are rattling around in your mind a constant barrage of poverty-talk, you must reframe those thoughts. Ideally, you will clear these beliefs at the level of the subconscious mind, but even if you don't or if it takes time, you can and must choose to hold thoughts that support your vision of wealth. Hold thoughts that support your being rich. Really see the Mercedes-Benz when you think of it. Daydreaming is allowed! The subconscious mind responds to visual and emotional stimuli. See it, know you have it, believe you have it, and think you have it. Amplify the Law of Attraction by using the rules of the mind. Build on all of this by truly living from a place of abundance, and you will achieve all that you desire.

If choosing to hold thoughts of abundance still feels like too much work to start, then at the very least get a handle on the repeating story you have running about money, and reframe those thoughts. I'm sure you must have friends whose mantra is, "I can't afford it!" If you are one of those people, you might start shifting by reframing, "I can't afford it" to "I am choosing to not spend my money on this at this time." It's all about getting yourself back into the driver's seat, so all those limiting beliefs stop informing every choice you make or how you feel whenever you spend money.

Just like with health and relationships, you can take control of your finances and generate wealth instead of constantly succumbing to circumstance and feeling victim to a system that is inarguably tilted in favor of the wealthy. You *are* the "Other people." The sooner you believe that you can change, that you have Universal Power within you to help generate change, that you can truly create your life the way you want it to be, the sooner you will be living in your own life masterpiece.

You can pinpoint and eradicate your limiting beliefs. You can use awareness and focus to choose to hold positive, abundant thoughts in place of any thought that comes from a place of lack or scarcity. You can reframe how you see yourself in the world to become more about what you can give, and how you can serve others, as opposed to solely coming from, "What's in it for me?" Making time to feel grateful for everything you have in your life - money, love, your dog, your health, the sunset, getting that parking spot so you weren't late for your meeting, anything and everything you are grateful for - assures more goodness to come your way. The world is abundant; whether or not you choose to live in and play in its abundance is entirely up to you. When you do decide to step into what is truly available for you, you can be sure that the Universal Power accessed through your subconscious mind will help you to make your desires a reality.

To contact Jim:

info@lutesinternational.com

www.lutesinternational.com

www.jimluteslive.com

Tom Hopkins

Tom Hopkins is world-renowned as "The Builder of Sales Champions." After setting sales records that were unbroken for decades, Tom launched a company that has trained over five million sales professionals and entrepreneurs on five continents. Tom teaches proven, practical communication skills for sales people and entrepreneurs as well as sales management strategies.

His entertaining style of delivery and simple, yet powerful strategies laid the foundation of some of the most successful sales careers ever - people who have generated billions of dollars in sales of products ranging from vitamins to corporate jets, insurance to cemetery services.

Tom is the author of 18 books on the subjects of selling and success including, *How to Master the Art of Selling*, *Selling for Dummies*, and *When Buyers Say No*. His training is also available through online courses, audio recordings, videos, and via seminars.

Tom's specialty is in customizing his proven-effective selling strategies and tactics for industry associations or for private companies. His goal is to provide such in-depth training that your sales team asks, "When did Tom work for us?" No one understands selling better than Tom Hopkins.

Before You Can Strive For Success, You Must Define It!

By Tom Hopkins

At the age of six, Corinne Archer* started putting in long hours training for her sport. She just loved it and discovered that she was really good at it. Long before she entered her teens, she had fixed her mind on a single goal: To win an Olympic gold medal.

From then on, she crushed everything out of her life that didn't contribute to her goal. Every available hour went to practice and perfecting her skills. As the years went by, she excelled in various competitions. Trophies and honors piled up, but they meant little to Corinne beyond making her dream of winning the gold medal seem a little more real. Each acknowledgement of her talent and skill made her work harder to become the very best in the world - that Olympic goal medalist.

After eleven years, the big day finally came, and Corinne Archer arrived at the Olympics to meet the world's toughest competitors. The contest was grueling, but she took first place. At seventeen, Corinne stood at the highest pinnacle she could ever hope to attain by her own definition of success. The gold medal, whose pursuit had dominated two-thirds of this young woman's life, was now hers.

Corrine left the victory stand in tears - of joy, or so everyone thought. For days, she was near tears much of the time. Unable to remember a time when every waking moment hadn't been driven by the demands of her formidable quest, Corinne realized almost at the instant of victory that she faced a blank future. She had no idea what to do next - no other goals to pursue.

Without her quest for gold, this intense young lady felt that she no longer had a purpose in life. From always living in the future, Corinne was suddenly jarred by the realization that her one great goal was now in the past. She still loved the sport and the competition, but what more was there to strive for? She had already proved that she was the best.

Corrine Archer sunk into a tremendous state of depression. Slowly, painfully, months went by. Then, she began to recover from the enormous emotional shock of losing her one goal by winning it. Corinne learned to live in the present, and to stop identifying herself solely by her expertise in that one sport.

Previously, Corinne had defined success as a single objective. Eventually, she learned the importance of having balance in life, and in having more than a single goal to strive toward. Without going into great detail, the rest of Corrine's life did come into balance and she has been successful in many endeavors.

Her story is important to all of us. Being singularly-focused is fine when striving for greatness in one area of your life. However, it's important to maintain perspective regarding the big picture of our whole lives. Perhaps Corinne was too young to understand that at the time she set and worked so hard for her goal. She certainly learned the lesson the hard way.

Success is Personal

Success doesn't have to be about winning medals or earning a specific income. There are plenty of people in the world who deem themselves successful after winning silver or bronze medals. Others enjoyed the experience of success just by making the Olympic team even though they didn't win any medals. Even more call themselves successful who developed into good, strong athletes yet never even competed with a potential Olympian. The point is that the term "success" means different things to different people. The important thing is to define what success means to you. Then, act in such a manner as to achieve that very personal definition of success.

I've had the good fortune of teaching entrepreneurs and sales professionals the world over. At many of my programs, I ask people the same question: "What does success mean to you?" I walk out into the audience with a microphone to get their answers. I almost always hear general answers such as: having money, taking great vacations, paying off the house, getting a new car and retiring early, but rarely will two people in the audience give me exactly the same answer.

Success is personal. The mental picture I see in my mind when I think of that word is not the same as what comes to mind for my wife, my sister, or my children. We are unique individuals with individual wants and needs.

We may even experience the same situations in life, but respond to them differently. Think about the stories of children raised in very positive environments who took very different paths as they grew up. There are plenty of stories about the opposite type of situation. How many of today's top athletes used their talents to help them rise up from poverty or overcome other great challenges in life? A lot. The question that remains is, "Why didn't their siblings do the same?" Because we all respond differently to the events in our lives.

This is why police officers prefer to speak with several witnesses to a crime or an accident instead of a single witness. Each person has their own perspective on what happened and can contribute different information to help in the investigation. For example, someone who is very attuned to fashion might be able to identify the brand of clothing the person was wearing where another witness couldn't even tell you the color of their clothing. Another person might be a hair stylist and be very specific about the haircut of the person. Someone who is into cars may have recognized the exact make, model, and year of the vehicle. We all see the world from different perspectives. So why should success be the same for everyone? It shouldn't.

Defining Success

Success is not just a thing we win, a place we arrive at, or a record we set. It's not just the numbers in our bank account, the address we live at, or the position we hold. In my mind, success is more than that. In fact, early in my own self-development education I created a definition of success for me. If it resonates with you, adopt it as your own. If it doesn't, that's okay, but I strongly advise you to invest your time in coming up with a definition that *does* work for you.

Before you can strive for success, you *must* define it. Otherwise, how will you know what steps you need to take in order to achieve it? How will you know when you've arrived?

My definition of success is as follows:

Success is the continuous journey toward the achievement of pre-determined, worthwhile goals.

Let me explain why those words work for me so you can create your own definition. The *continuous journey* reminds me that I'm not finished achieving until my life is over. I'm sure you've heard that every experience you've ever had in life has contributed to the person you've become thus far. Is who you are today good enough? Or, do you aspire to even more greatness in some areas of your life?

As human beings, we have opportunities to grow, develop, and change every day of our lives - even if it's just in how we think. And, how we invest our time along our journey each and every day makes a positive or negative impact on the end result we'll get.

Since our lives are realities that go on and on, true success, the kind that doesn't crumble into dust the moment we get our hands on it, must be part of that continuous journey. Each goal you set and strive for moves you toward its achievement.

Let's say you think you'll be a success when you have a million dollars in the bank at your chosen retirement age. That may be the defining moment in time against where you'll make a measurement, but every dollar contributed to the account along the way is what makes the end result what it is. Each dollar is a part of the journey toward that million dollars. Every step *toward the achievement* of whatever success means to you is a successful step in your journey.

In order to achieve the end result of your definition of success, choose specific goals and break them down into the daily habits and actions you take. *Predetermine* them far enough in advance of their deadlines to allow yourself to change and grow enough to achieve them. The great modern day philosopher Jim Rohn said, "Set a goal to become a millionaire, not for the money, but for what it makes of you to achieve it." I agree.

Predetermine what you want your life to be like in 20 years. Look around you. Who do you know that is 20 years older than you? What aspects of their personalities, lifestyles, and achievements do you admire? What aspects of their lives do you want to have in your own? Write them down. Look them over. Then, ask yourself if you deem them to be *worthwhile* enough for you to invest your time and effort in achieving them.

Worthwhile is the next word in my definition.

Nothing that will give lasting satisfaction can be achieved unless the goals striven for are *worthwhile*. We just won't keep putting forth the energy and effort required to achieve something that we don't believe is 100% worthwhile. That's just human nature.

Discovering and moving toward what is truly worthwhile *to you* is the most challenging and rewarding task of your *continuous journey* through life. What *is* worthwhile to you? Is it the satisfaction of sailing around the world in your own yacht? Or, is it scuttling around the local lake in a kayak? It doesn't matter what *it* is as long as it's important to you - and will bring you a sense of achievement. What does matter is that you choose the direction of your life - that you take action toward achieving success rather than letting time slip by and having not enough of it left in life to be, do, and have what you want.

Keeping it all in Balance

Little Corinne, was totally out of balance by only having one goal, wasn't she? While hyper-focus might get you where you want to go in a single endeavor faster, being out of balance might have you arrive at success with no one to share the joy.

When I was quite young, I set a goal to become a millionaire by the age of 30. I learned new skills. I worked more hours that most of my peers. I conducted more business than ever before in my career. I purposely lived a life out of balance in order to achieve my goal. I didn't spend as much time with my family as others in my field. However, I included my family in my goals. They understood that my rewards for working so hard would also be beneficial to them. They supported me when I had rough days. They inspired me to keep going, and we celebrated together.

I achieved the status of having a million dollars of net worth by the age of 27 - beating my goal by three whole years. If I hadn't understood and acted on my knowledge of goals, I could have been in rough shape, like Corinne, but for three years - wondering what to do with myself between the ages of 27 and 30.

I've seen it happen all too often. People put everything they've got into their careers in order to make money to provide a bigger house or better vacations for their families. They work late at night. They work weekends. They're constantly checking their work email on their phones. The big financial payoff comes but at what price? The loved ones they were working for don't know them anymore. They've missed too many family dinners, soccer games, and even birthday parties.

Direct your efforts toward achieving a successful *life* - not just a successful career. Only you can define precisely what achieving a successful life means to you. But, if happiness has any place in your set of values, your successful life will probe many interests, experience many emotions, fill many needs, and accomplish many aims.

I strongly recommend that you begin with goals for your health - physical fitness. After all, getting rich at the cost of your health is not a good plan. I'm not saying wealth isn't worthwhile. Do set goals for wealth - for financial independence - but wealth you can acquire without killing yourself to do it.

Set goals that positively impact your emotional stability. This includes continually learning and growing mentally. I know of a man who in his late 70's would often say, "Today was a good day...

I learned something new." Be open in both mind and heart to new experiences every day.

And, last, but not least by any means, set goals for spiritual fulfillment in order to achieve and maintain a good sense of balance within. You'll have to create your own definition for spiritual fulfillment, too. It's different for each person on this earth. Just don't ignore this aspect if you're committed to living your life in balance.

Success isn't all of the sudden. Success is every day. Once you get near your current goals, start thinking about where you'll go after you get there. This is vital. And you can do it without diverting energy from nailing down the great success you're closing in on now. Before achieving each aim, rest your mind occasionally by speculating on what your next goals will be. Make a written list of your ideas. As you find free moments, collect your thoughts about your new goals. Gather information on them.

Be prepared to plunge into the pursuit of new goals as soon as you celebrate your current goals. Unless you do that, you'll get bored. You'll get depressed. Witness the number of people who earn celebrity and wealth in show business and then lose everything to alcohol or drugs. By envisioning your life as a continuous journey toward the achievement of pre-determined, worthwhile goals, you'll constantly be learning new things, seeing things in new ways, and experiencing great joy in life.

Define what success means to you. Then, hop on the path in its direction - enjoying every step of the journey.

Footnote: *Not her real name.

To contact Tom:

Tom Hopkins International, Inc.

465 E Chilton Drive, Suite 4

Chandler, Arizona USA 85225

tomh@tomhopkins.com

(480) 949-0786

Sample his training at www.tomhopkins.com/blog

Hara Taicher

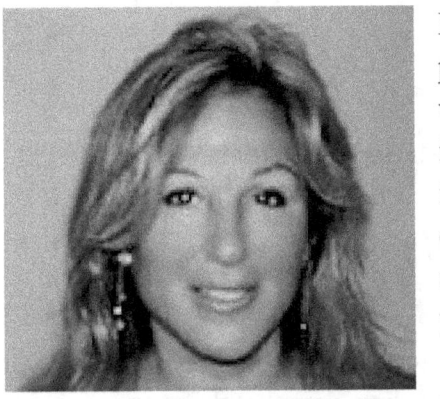

Hara Taicher is an author, personal development coach, as well as an engaging and inspirational speaker. Her topics include self-empowerment, effective communications skills and how to identify and achieve your dreams.

As a coach, Hara inspires you to be your very best. She commits to provide you the unconditional support and encouragement to attain your goals and mastery in any area of life.

Hara's clients discover how to navigate their personal landscape to achieve their goals, bring clarity to the decision making processes, enhance personal and professional relationships, find choice where none seemed to exist and free them from the limitations of the past.

Your Personal GPS Guide to Positive Change

By Hara Taicher

I've spent a good part of my life repeating the same mistakes over and over again. What I didn't know then, was that there was an inner blueprint embedded deep in my subconscious mind that was literally controlling my life and affecting the outcome of everything I did.

All throughout my 20's and 30's I poked around self-help books, but it wasn't until after the birth of my son, going through a divorce and back to living on my own again, that I began to really immerse myself into self-empowerment.

As a single mom, re-entering the workforce and dating again, I found out very quickly that some things were not as I expected. I didn't understand why I wasn't achieving what I set out to do. Every time I thought I was on my way to finding my path to success, I would lose steam or hit a dead end.

I finally had ENOUGH! Enough disappointments and enough of 'almost' getting there. It was then I decided to study with some of the top spiritual/success trainers who would show me how to rescue my mind from self-imposed limitations and master the laws of manifestation.

What I discovered were powerful tools, exercises and strategies that taught me how to access the unconscious mind and reprogram the information stored there.

I discovered how to change my blueprint!

My exploration helped put me back in the driver's seat again. It totally transformed my life. I no longer dwelled on my disappointments. I had come to realize the subtle, yet powerful steps to manifesting, and how to navigate situations for positive outcomes.

If you're experiencing frustration and challenges, if you don't know why they keep happening and how to overcome them, then this personal GPS guide can offer valuable insights to steer you in the right direction. In fact, from my own personal experience I can tell you that by employing this mindset, you can start achieving faster, and more abundantly than ever before.

What if there was a way to have it all? What if there was a secret way to 'be' that was like a giant magnet attracting the good and fulfilling things to you?

What if the most powerful tool you have to achieve this is in the way you think? And by listening to the thoughts you are thinking and the words you are speaking, you would be able to identify the reason you are not attaining what you want. Then, by being able to pin point this information, you could begin taking certain actions to implement corrections so that you are able to manifest your desires.

It would follow that you would be on an unstoppable course.

In this chapter, I will reveal steps for unraveling information stored in the conscious and unconscious mind.

I hope that my life experiences will help to expedite your journey so that you can begin today, right here and now, to feel relief from whatever is keeping you from realizing a creative and fulfilling life and to start feeling powerful again.

If you are seeking guidance to assist you in changing your thinking so your life can change, then this just might be the 'corner' piece of the puzzle that can help you find some answers. I believe that once you're ready and willing to make changes in your life, once you're in alignment with your aspirations and are focused... the Universe, like an overnight delivery, will provide you with the information you need to fulfill your life's desires.

It's time to embark on your journey and learn how to unravel your blueprint and unleash your inner navigator.

Now, press the pedal to the metal and let's begin!

"We are all here for some special reason. Stop being a prisoner of your past. Become the architect of your future." - Robin Dharma

You Can't Pack Your Bags, If Your Suitcase Is Already Full

Ok, so you're ready to go on a transformational road trip. What do you need to do first? Get the suitcase out and begin packing. Only thing is, when you open your bag, you find that it's completely FULL! It's full of old unproductive thoughts and beliefs that you've been carrying around. It's loaded with your baggage from the past, why things haven't worked out... your STORY.

You know, the tale you tell about why you're in the situation you're in. Why you can't move forward... what you should have done, what opportunities you've missed... all of it.

Your story is just a conversation in your head that you keep repeating over and over again. In some ways, it has defined you. In truth, it has limited you.

Just like those 'old clothes' that need to be thrown out of your closet, achieving a positive shift requires you to unpack your negative thoughts and discard what doesn't 'fit.'

Liberating yourself from your STORY is one of the most important steps to change your thinking. Dragging it into your present conversations, only serves to recreate it.

We become so attached to repeating our story that it has become our calling card. Everyone knows your woeful tale… probably by heart. Even if you're not consciously doing this, when you take time to really break down why things aren't working, it's a good chance the counter-productive, underlying emotional attachments you have to your past are the cause. They're part of what's keeping you stuck.

Your thoughts of what's happened to you in the past are really just re-enactments of events. Those events are imbued with emotions that were present at the time of the experience. So the past is really like a diary of events.

The negative emotions you have surrounding those events are what you need to deal with, because they are showing up in present day, affecting your reality. They need to be explored to examine what caused them in the first place.

A good exercise is to revisit a negative experience when you are feeling relaxed, and your emotional energy about what happened has subsided. When looking at the situation from that unattached perspective, do those feelings affect you in the same way? Would you have the same reaction if the experience were to take place in the present?

Think about it. Your emotional state at the time a negative experience happened may have been affected by any number of things that contributed to your reaction. Isn't it possible that if that same situation were to have occurred when you were feeling productive and self-assured, you might not have reacted in the same way?

Unchecked negative emotions are really the culprit here. Our feelings can distort reality, blow them out of proportion and alter our interpretation. Staying stuck in a negative memory is a choice. We either dwell on it or we move on.

Reliving our disappointments, when things didn't go our way or how we envisioned them is another self-made roadblock.

Everyone on this planet has experienced disappointments and setbacks. Harrison Ford was fired from Columbia Pictures and told he would never make it. Woody Allen was thrown out of NYU when he was studying to be a filmmaker. The Beatles were rejected by Decca Recording Company. They didn't like their sound!

Setbacks, disappointments and frustrations are a part of life. It's how you deal with them and the attitude you employ that will make them either traumatic or just another 'learning' bump in the road on the way to your goal.

Don't try to make changes all at once. Take one step at a time. Letting go of old unproductive ways of being is very powerful.

As you go through the items in your bag, take a moment and ask yourself, "Do I really need this anymore?" If the answer is NO, then toss it OUT!

It's time to reprogram your GPS… you're heading in a new direction!

> *"You can't solve a problem with the same thinking that got you into the problem."* - Albert Einstein

You'll Need To Fasten Your Seat Belt... It Could Be a Bumpy Ride!

When going on a trip, it's a good idea to be open to new possibilities. Plans change. You decide somewhere along the way that you want to take a different route. There's some place that looks really interesting that you didn't know about before and you'd really like to take the time to explore. So you detour off the course to take the scenic drive. It's the same process as we begin to review where we are in life and where we are choosing to go. First we look at our starting point, where we are in the present and then start to plot out a path to begin.

All along the way on this transformational journey, we will be confronted with the necessity to change. There is no escaping that fact! For most, that's easier said than done.

What is the first step to making a change?

Awareness. You have to consciously realize that something doesn't feel right and then look for solutions to make it better.

You might have noticed that you've been stuck in the same thought process for far too long, but just don't know what to do about it.

Why is it so challenging for people to make changes?

Habits are powerful. You get used to doing things in a certain way. You know what to expect from the things that you do and although they may not be producing the results you desire, it's in your comfort zone to know what's expected of you, so your awareness remains status quo.

Fear of the unknown. It's uncomfortable to go where you haven't been.

You don't know what it is that needs changing. Have you ever wracked your brain trying to figure out just what it is that keeps holding you back, but you haven't a clue on how to move forward?

That's the thing about change. There are things that you are aware of and other things you have no idea about. These are conscious and unconscious behaviors. On a conscious level, you can examine experiences and do whatever work you choose to repair the situation. But when it comes to the unconscious, if it's something you don't know and are unaware of, how can you possibly do any work to make it better?

For many years, I was working on the things I knew needed changing. If I had an unresolved problem, I went to workshops and seminars that dealt with clearing those issues. As much as those exercises would shift my thinking and allow for new thoughts to come through, there would always seem to be something else that needed to be done. I would be exhausted trying to figure out what in the world I was missing. I spent so much time in the healing process regarding my past relationships that I couldn't believe it when I'd hit that proverbial bump in the road again. Hadn't I resolved this already? After all, I thought, "How much time can a person devote to working on the same issue? Doesn't there just come a point when you're done? Wasn't there a reward for sheer effort that bumped you to the finish line?"

What I discovered was that all those seminars were only a superficial fix. There was more to all of this that no one told me about. I was coming from a place of logic. My rational mind was looking at my current situation and evaluating what needed to be done.

My logical mind could only help me so much. It was then I realized that I also had to get in touch with… my feelings.

As it turns out, our emotions provide us with a valuable source of information. Even 'negative' emotions can give us powerful guidance. When we are feeling angry or depressed, frustrated or overwhelmed, these types of emotions are clear indicators that we are disconnected. Paying attention to your feelings can give you some important answers to why you are stuck, how you got there and why you continue to stay there.

You know what that means?

It's time for a tune-up. We're going to need to get under the hood!

"We are like magnets. You become AND attract what you think." - The Secret

Rules Of The Road… Thoughts, Feelings and The Law of Attraction

When our thoughts and feelings are compatible with each other, we attain the perfect environment for creating. When we are not getting what we desire, it is because one or both of those elements is out of whack. This is The Law of Attraction. It states that anything like itself is attracted to itself. Like attracts like. Example: If you harp on negative things, more negative things will be attracted to you. A cosmic boomerang!

There's no getting around this law, so you might as well try to understand all the nuances of it and to use it wisely. It's operating whether you are aware of it or not!

Commonly, people using this law only focused on what they were thinking. Their interpretation of the law was that if one thinks good thoughts, good things would come to you. But as its popularity grew and more people began to apply this to their lives, they were disappointed that they were not experiencing the breakthroughs that were promised. What they didn't know, was that a very important piece of the equation was missing.

An even more powerful part of the process was to connect with your true feelings. When you are in touch with your feelings, they can become one of your most productive and fulfilling assets to understand the cause of your behavior.

Think of it like this... your logical mind is the last to know. Your feelings, whether you are aware of them or not, are the subconscious originators of your behavior.

If you ask yourself questions about a situation with which you are uncomfortable and causes you emotional pain, you may come to realize that underneath your conversation, is a wealth of clues to better understand yourself.

Hold on to the steering wheel... there's a sharp turn ahead!

"If you fail to plant desires into your subconscious mind, it will feed upon the thoughts which reach it as a result of your neglect." - Napoleon Hill

There Are NO Accidents!

Even if you're a good driver there is always the chance of an unforeseen incident. After all, there are other people on the road that require your attention. You are interacting with them just as you interact with people in your daily life.

When other people swerve into your lane, without signaling, you have no warning. You have to react quickly to maneuver your vehicle safely. The same circumstances apply to your life. There will be times when an unforeseen challenge presents itself.

Unforeseen can be interpreted as your 'blind spot,' where experiences just show up out of nowhere and you can't see them even when they're right next to you. Your blind spots are your unconscious beliefs. You can't see them and more importantly, you know little, if anything about them. They are unconscious and they manifest themselves in unpredictable ways. So even when you act diligently to monitor your thoughts and actions, it doesn't mean you're not going to uncover some unexpected rough emotional roads to navigate.

What is happening is, your old programming is now being revamped with new information. It doesn't just all fall into place. In fact, as you apply these new behaviors, you might experience contrasting behaviors as well.

Why?

It's part of the releasing process. What needs to be released are the unconscious counter intentions that are deeply embedded in the subconscious mind. As you begin to get into a new program, fortified with good thoughts and positive vibes, evidence of stuck thinking will start to surface.

90% of our actions are an unconscious mystery to us, which obviously means we are only aware of 10%! That's got to lead to some serious questions about what the other 90% is up to!

What activates those unconscious behaviors? Is there a way to begin deciphering some of the information stored there?

I'm glad you asked!

We have a belief that our conscious mind is directing our lives. We say things like, "This is what I want to achieve in life" or "I want to do things that are meaningful and extraordinary!" Yet many times, the end result doesn't match our intentions.

That's because it's our <u>limiting and self-sabotaging sub-conscious programs</u> that are really running the show!

What programs will that subconscious mind run? The programs that were originally downloaded. All the thoughts and behaviors you learned as a child. The only way to change those old tapes is to go into the subconscious mind and rewrite the program.

All thoughts are powerful, especially the ones you are unaware of.

Your subconscious mind is an intricate and deep-rooted collection of beliefs that are wielding an extremely powerful magnetic force in your life. When there is no interference, i.e., your subconscious thoughts are in alignment with what you consciously desire, you will attract it. But if there are thoughts and beliefs that are in conflict with what you are consciously desiring - you will not achieve the results you want.

The most important thing to understand is that because these behaviors are so deeply rooted in our subconscious mind, this will be a part of your life that will always require your attention. "There is no finish line with the unconscious mind." As you develop a clearer picture of yourself, you will be confronted with new challenges that will require you to always be 'checking in.'

Barriers to your goal are going to show up but instead of surrendering in frustration, realize they are showing you what you need to pay attention to. They are pointing you in the direction of what still needs to be cleared so that you can effectively deal with it and then just let it GO!

That means you're making progress!

Whatever the realization might be, the result is profound and YOU are finally in charge!

Starting the day off aligning your inner self with affirming behaviors will build a habit of positive conviction and abundance.

Then the road then on which you travel will no longer be full of emotional potholes but instead, the road will support and enrich you.

"We are what we repeatedly do. Excellence, then, is not an act but a habit." - Aristotle

Revving Your Engine (Conditioning the Mind For Success)

Why is it that people don't follow through on their desires? Why do they allow themselves to stay stuck in negativity even though they know it's one of the biggest deterrents in achieving their goals? It is because thoughts are so powerful. When you continue to think the same thoughts over and over, they become deeply ingrained habits. It's as though your negative thinking is on autopilot!

Do you ever wonder why people think in such a negative way? They may tell you that they are not negative… they are realistic. They don't even bother to look at the belief system they've adopted. They believe what they believe and in their minds, that is the truth.

If our beliefs are rooted in lack, limitation and negativity, then it is for sure we will end up sourcing elements of lack in whatever we're attempting to create. What happens is when we execute a plan, we do so with less than 100% certainty that we will achieve our goal. Our subliminal mindset negatively affects our results.

Think about it. If you set out to accomplish something but you don't really believe you can do it, then any action you take to reach that goal will be half-hearted, and as a result, your outcome will be diminished. You think you won't be able to do something, but you try anyway. Your efforts are in line with your self-doubt. They don't have the impact of complete certainty. When you don't get the results you were after, you can console yourself by saying, "I knew this would happen!"

When you enter into something with a thought of anything less than "I'm going to give 100% of my effort," the end result is proportionate to the percentage you've put in. And while there is a lot to be said about trying, why not expect the best results.

Everything in this world has a magnetic frequency to it, including 'your thoughts.' This vibration is being sent out in everything you do. It's like your own personal radio station that is broadcasting your thoughts.

So, if you attempted something with an "I'll give it a try" attitude, your actions are going to reflect unsure thinking. The word 'try' implies that you may be able to and then again, you may not. With that kind of thinking, your results will end up being a mutation of your goal. You didn't get what you wanted, which reinforced your original thought that success was doubtful at best. You actually proved yourself right!

That's a self-fulfilling prophecy!

What is it that creates absolute certainty that you can do something? Getting your belief in alignment with your goal. You can do this by 'pre-paving.' See or imagine what you want to achieve for the day, in your mind. It's good to do it first thing in the morning, as it paves the way for the days' experiences. When your mind sees a positive result over and over again, it becomes conditioned to expect that outcome.

How much does the mind effect performance? Tony Robbins did a study with NBA players. He had three groups. One group practiced making free throws all the time. The second group didn't practice at all. The third group visualized making the free throws. Group number three excelled. Those who pre-paved had absolute certainty. They saw themselves making the shot every time. The mental practicing they did helped them to release whatever block they had that was causing them not to make the shot.

In the visualization exercise, many issues can come up but once you work through them, you can release them! Then there is no interference. There are no excuses.

When you think about it, what is reality? It's our perception! Practicing is not enough. Visualizing prepares the mind to be accustomed to success.

Once you start paying attention to what it is you're thinking and speaking about... Once you deliberately choose positive behaviors over negative... Once you make a "what you want to have happen" list to get your mind organized... Once you commit your mind to a program of conditioning for results...

Your suitcase will be packed with new ways of being and your success is going to skyrocket!

"Great things are not done by impulse, but by a series of small things brought together." - Vincent Van Gogh

So It Really Is The Journey, Not The Destination After All

We've covered a lot of territory in this transformational road trip. We've let go of old ways of thinking and being, and have gained some new insights and new tools to recreate ourselves. It's exciting!

Changing your thinking begins the process for your life to change. We've gone quite a distance to get new thoughts, ideas and strategies that can bring you to the positive side of any unproductive thoughts, and can shed some light on behaviors you've been wanting to transform.

Always be open to new realizations, so that every day you grow and your awareness expands.

One thing is for sure, whatever situations arise, employing a positive attitude, complete with a reality check of your feelings, will land you on the super highway of life.

One day your life will pass before your eyes. Make sure it's worth watching!

To contact Hara:

www.getcenteredwithhara.com

(212) 753-9590

Leigh Adams, DTM, QS

November 27, 2004, I retired after being diagnosed with stage 4 colon cancer. I'm blessed to be here after 9 operations and approximately 90 rounds of chemo. I walked away from a very successful business to find my new purpose in life, how to love cancer and help it find its way out of me.

I've been involved in Toastmasters since 2009.

I had a retail business since 1984 that had between 50 and 120 employees that was doing in excess of $14 million a year in consumer electronics, from one single 5000 square foot store in Ontario, California. We invented selling consumer electronics, at the LA County fair. In 18 days, we did an excess of $2 million with 50 sales people that had no selling experience.

I have served on many boards: United Way, Upland Police Foundation, Mitsubishi, LG, Panasonic and Pioneer as the number one/two dealer in the world.

Coach/consultant for Zig Ziglar, Wilson Learning, Bob Proctor and others.

Find A Way to Move Forward

By Leigh Adams, DTM, QS

"Gunshots coming at us!" Sam yells, "Hit the ground!" We all start firing our guns above our heads, trying to hit something... scared out of our minds. John pokes his head through the bushes and hears a few shots whiz past his left. When he hollers, "11:00!" everyone starts shooting with everything they have. Sam springs up, runs ahead in a zigzag pattern and throws a grenade with all his strength. Suddenly, the gunshots stop. Everything is silent. We hear crickets starting to sing. We see mosquitoes flying around us, and we swat at them. The smell of gunpowder, fire, and smoke fills our senses. We are still waiting patiently as we feel our hearts beating rapidly. We slowly start walking towards the battle scene. We hear a slight rustle from a nearby bush. We stop in our tracks. We wait... thump... thump... our hearts and instincts tell us something is approaching. We stand there paralyzed and shaking with fear, all of our senses firing, not knowing what might come next. Suddenly, out of a bush, a little black puppy shows up. We all smile and it takes our minds away from the hell we just went through.

Even in hell we can all find things to appreciate, and we can also envision a better place. In Victor Frankl's book, *Man's Search for Meaning,* we can read about survivors of the Holocaust who imagined themselves alive in the future, to tell what happened. Even in the present, no matter how bad it is, we can always make things better. Sometimes a bomb goes off and shatters the course of our life. Everyone experiences this, and everyone who succeeds doubts themselves at times and have no idea how to accomplish their goals. If we concentrate on what we want and look for the opportunities in everything that's bad, we can discover how extraordinary we are. People whose experience and perspective is different from our own can give us far more power and leverage than we ever can achieve alone. In 2004, a traumatic event gave me a new purpose in life. It would change my life forever. Let me explain how my first job as a cook at Carl's Jr. in 1972, while I was going to college as a music major, was very instrumental in my thinking.

At the end of the second week as a cook at Carl's Jr., the manager was hollering "go faster," in front of dozens of customers and the four cashiers taking orders. There were over twenty-five orders for hamburgers and I couldn't keep up. I stopped, took a step back and noticed the others working to fill the orders. They were waiting... for me to call out the orders, and were just standing around. I took it all in. The manager was hollering at me, "What are you doing?" I was trying to understand the whole process and figure out how to be more efficient. When the lunch rush was over, the manager was so angry, she ordered me out of the restaurant and told me if I ever did that again, I'd be fired! I asked if I could take the policy and procedures manual home to study. Her reply was, "Absolutely NOT! Now, get OUT!" I took the manual home anyway and decided I was going to figure out a better way. I was in such gratitude for the position and wanted to show my appreciation. Why not try and make my job fun, efficient and more fulfilling.

My father had told me I needed to learn how to be a great follower, because that was important to being a leader. My goal was to figure out how to make the cook's positions easier and more efficient, as well as the rest of the team love their roles. I couldn't get fired. I needed money to eat and live in my small apartment, furnished only with my sleeping bag.

I spent the rest of the day and night attempting to make sense of things and come up with a more efficient procedure. When I came in the next morning, my manager fired me. Luckily, one of the founder's family members, who worked in my store, took my proposal to Carl and Don Karcher (his uncle and father). Their main office was behind our store and Carl Karcher ran out and stopped me from leaving. He told me my proposal was genius. I kept my job and was promoted to manager trainee that day. Carl's Jr. training exposed me to Jim Rohn, Zig Ziglar, and many others who are some of the greatest leaders of today. I succeeded in designing a more efficient way to take orders, which sped up the time to deliver them by almost a minute, and helped grow the company. I worked at this incredible company for seven years inventing many things and learned how to run a company, as I moved up from Manager to District Manager.

Even in terrible situations in life, you can free yourself from the painful grip circumstances will have on you if you focus on how to make it better rather than complaining or dwelling in bitterness, frustration or anger. This was a huge lesson for me. My life today, running a business efficiently, was mostly because of my time with Carl's Jr.. Thank you Carl!

After spending three days with Jim Rohn, from the age of nineteen on, I would study every bit of sales material and personal development I could get my hands on. I discovered rapid growth by forming mastermind groups, thanks to Napoleon Hill's *Think and Grow Rich*. I dove into books, tapes, courses, seminars, and invested tens of thousands of dollars to learn. I always had second jobs while at Carl's, to learn about different skills, industries, to make more money and find out how the business world operated. My Carl's career came first always! I had two MLM businesses, a tax preparers business with over 300 clients and 60 companies, got my Real Estate license, a contractor's license to find out what I loved to do and make money. My appetite for knowledge allowed me to take struggling retail companies, business-to-business, wholesale, and other industries doing five or six figures a year, to eight and nine figures per year. I had my first coaching client, a restaurant chain, at twenty years old. Within a month, they made more money than they ever had made in a year. To do this, I used principles I had learned from Jim Rohn and Carl's Jr.. Despite this success, I still did not have the confidence or self-image to go into business for myself. When an opportunity to buy a restaurant came, I was too afraid to do it on my own, and didn't want to be an owner without having complete control, especially if I was doing all the work. I also didn't want to have investors or partners telling me how to run it and have them be in control.

I decided to get a job involving something I love, home audio and video. I was already selling equipment on the side. I went to work as a retail salesman, then moved up to Vice President of Sales and Marketing in a consumer electronics store. I grew the company twenty-fold in three years but couldn't make enough money. I was paid a percentage of net profit. Even though we were profitable, the owner deducted so many large and luxurious personal purchases through the business, there was no profit to show. When I left, he gave me one of his Mercedes as back pay.

I then worked for a major financial services company promising huge money and an opportunity to learn finance. I started as a salesman and moved up to Vice President rapidly, where I had a mission to hire and train the best salespeople. As much as I needed to make more money at that time, I could never have anticipated this would take the form of a large pay cut.

It was suggested Al Tomsik would make a great salesman at the financial company. During the interview, he offered me the chance to work with him for free. I laughed and said that I would check him out. I called my brother Chris, who was the top performing sales person along with Tony Robbins, for Jim Rohn's seminars at the time. Chris said that Al Tomsik was one of the greatest salesman in the world and that even as a leader in the Mormon Church, Al had never allowed a person to work for him despite many approaches. Al personally coached over 800 of the top companies in the US, implementing sales processes and strategies. He ended up selling me on the idea of quitting my job to work for free until I could get on the stage. From that moment on, I spent every waking moment studying him. Al had a video training course that was $6,000 in 1980. I learned how to sell real estate franchises and list and sell houses with all of his material, which is what he was working on at the time. I had to meet his standards before I could ever train how to sell and coach in any business on my own.

One morning I went to his house in Irvine to prepare for my first moment on stage in front of about 400 people that afternoon. I was so excited to finally be able to use the skills I had honed. As I pulled up to his home, red flashing lights lit up the neighborhood. My stomach turned when I realized the ambulance and fire trucks were there for Al. He had died in his sleep. At 62, he was as healthy as could be. Now he was gone. I crushed and tearfully hugged Mrs. Tomsik. She told me, "He went to a better place knowing he finally found someone who could carry on his work." She asked me to do this, but I thought, "Who am I to think I can replace Al? I don't have what it takes." My self-image just wasn't there, so I never carried on his legacy the way she had hoped. Just like the restaurant opportunity, my self-image sabotaged me at every turn. Fortunately, the training and knowledge I received from Al was worth more than anything he could've paid me. Through his wisdom and teachings, I experienced tremendous growth following him and loved every minute of it.

After Al Tomsik, I returned to what I loved, getting a job as a salesman in a wholesale rep company selling consumer electronics. I wanted to learn how companies made money and figure out how to have my own business. I started out as a salesperson and moved up to trainer, then vice president of sales, and given a part of the company. I was finally part owner of a company. Shortly after, they went public and lost their two major lines and the company went into bankruptcy. This led me to buy a local consumer electronics store on the verge of closing.

Up to this point, you might be thinking that I excelled at everything in my life. So how can I say that anybody can change? Eventually, I achieved enormous financial independence, but the period up to when I bought my business was one of the toughest and least happy times in my life. I cried at night because I was not seeing my kids who lived 450 miles away with my ex-wife. I didn't know how I would afford to see them in the future, though I had the support of my new wife Paula, and always had at least two jobs or side businesses simultaneously. I was in my early thirties and had changed careers multiple times within a few years to make more money. I realized I couldn't keep leaving jobs and expect to be a provider, especially when most of my income went to child support. I never seemed to make enough money. Whenever I started to get close to my financial goals as a rep, my territory or my commission would get cut in half. This happened so many times that I worried about my future, my financial situation, and myself as a father. During the workday, I would escape to play video games just to get my mind off my problems. Though I was still the company's best performing sales rep and they were one of the largest consumer electronics distributors at the time, I was not allowed to earn more money. It became clear that I could not continue and had to go into business for myself. Luckily, I was able to find the cash without taking on an investor.

Both in retail and wholesale, I was constantly listening to what customers wanted. I had called on small accounts and national key accounts and saw their books. I understood why some were failing and succeeding and started to see a niche for myself. When I decided to buy my business, I sold the Mercedes. I had finally grown up and made a decision to live my dream!

However unprepared you feel, remember that *every successful person* had serious fears and insecurities before and *after* they got started on a major change. I knew I had all the reasons and tools to go into business for myself, but did not believe I could do it on my own because I never graduated from college. I never wanted to work by myself. I believed that I needed a support partner. I was afraid of a lot of things! Fear, worry, doubt and my poor self-image always got in my way.

In May of 1984, I bought a very small store in Upland, California, called Discount Sales. I started out simply asking, "What are my action steps to do today?" I joined Rotary, The Chamber of Commerce, networking clubs, and spent a year calling a minimum of 100 people every day from my target audience and found out what they wanted from a store. These were people living in the most expensive homes and earning over $100,000 per year. I recorded all of my customer interactions. My wife and I reviewed and studied our interactions daily and worked twelve to eighteen hours a day for a few years.

I began driving around in a Toyota pickup with boxes in the back, as though I were making deliveries, all to create the image of success. Many days and weeks there were no customers and calls. It was scary! My wife modeled and acted on the side to help pay for advertising. This allowed me to spend huge amounts of money advertising which created top of mind awareness, TOMA, with my local market and drove traffic to my store. At this point, you should realize that when I started, I was not special. I had serious self-doubts and insecurities. What I did do was work harder than anybody I knew and kept asking myself what I could do better and listen to what my customers wanted. I became a sales and personal development trainer for Zig Ziglar, Wilson Learning and Harry Friedman for my sales people. In my seventh month in business, I moved the store and finally made more money that first month than I ever made in a year. Location, Location! I never gave up! However, in 2004, twenty-five years later, my life took a dramatic turn.

On a rainy early morning, I lay awake, staring into the black space of our hotel room. The sun hadn't risen and I hadn't slept because my past year of mysterious stomach pains had just reached a climax. My son's high school cross country team was scheduled to leave our hotel to the California State Championship course in a few hours. My wife and I got ready and I jogged downstairs to breakfast, doing everything to get my mind off the mounting pain. When I sat down, I felt pressure release from my gut and was completely relieved for the first time. That's when I noticed my sweats were soaked, as blood ran down my legs and onto the floor. No one except my wife and doctor found out what happened that day until after I raced 300 miles to the hospital near my home… after watching my son perform, and against the recommendation of my doctor to get to the nearest ER.

I was scanned immediately and told a tumor in my blocked colon had ruptured and that I only have six to twelve months to live, and to get my things in order. Surgery was needed, but I wanted a second opinion to get a better idea of the extent of the cancer. The main doctor was not available, so another would have to do surgery immediately. I said, "No. I want to wait a day or two if necessary." I needed referrals from my personal doctor as to who the best surgeon was. I didn't want to hear a diagnosis from someone who had no idea of the extent of the cancer. Getting someone who could actually tell this from the surgery was the best I knew to do. We found a man who would turn out to be a blessing. Dr. Yamanishi operated on me the following day. After I came out of surgery, he told me how lucky I was to still have my colon, and that I had stage IV colon cancer which had spread throughout my liver and seven lymph nodes.

Later that night, I told my nurses, "I want to get up and walk." They refused! My response was, "I'm not going to sit here and wait. I need to get up and get my blood moving to heal myself." I was in strong physical condition from working out and running every day. When I started to get up, the nurses said, "We're going to strap you down." I said, "Please call the doctor, I want to get up." They didn't come back soon enough, so I decided to get up. I started unplugging everything. They came back and began strapping me down when the doctor called and told the nurses, "If he is going to be that determined to get up, then let him get up, just stay by his side." I HAD to get my blood moving. I truly believed this would get the healing process started. I walked for about five minutes. Two hours later I walked another five. After two more hours, another ten.

Early that morning Dr. Yamanishi came in smiling and shaking his head. He had a few words for me as he was laughing. I said, "Doc, I'm going to be the first person who gets healed from this. And it starts right now. So tell me what I have to do." Later, I would seek many second opinions and forms of coaching over the next ten years. A few of them would save my life just as they had always done for me in business.

When I met Dr. Yamanishi, my tiny 1000 sq ft store grossing less than $200,000 a year had grown into the second largest independent dealer of big screens and entertainment centers in the world. We grossed over $14 million per year, out of 5000 sq ft. I was working 20-30 hours a week in the store, eight months out of the year, with a $14.5 million business and a responsibility to over

50-120 employees, their families and 90,000 customers. Despite all this, my first responsibility was to get well. I never cried and never asked, "Why me?" I was entirely focused on getting well while my family and friends endlessly researched everything to help decide what was the best course of action.

It was one of the most powerful things in my life to realize during this time how lucky I was to have such loving family and friends. This gratitude pushed me through the most difficult times of my healing. Whenever we're in difficult situations, whether in our relationships, our business, or our health, we absolutely need to be aware of the good we have in our lives. The more we are grateful, the less room there is for any un-constructive, negative, fearful, or worrying thoughts. Gratitude is so powerful that it allows us to see solutions where we might otherwise only see problems and despair.

You can achieve your dreams if you have enough reasons burning inside. You probably won't know how to get them, but ask yourself, "Am I able to do it and am I willing to do it?" You can achieve your dreams with sheer willpower and faith. The big problems you face on your journey often provide the greatest opportunity to learn and do something extraordinary. To eliminate or minimize mistakes, save time and money by seeking other people's expertise, feedback and mentorship. Find a coach or mentor and get into a mastermind group and discover for yourself why they are powerful. Learn how to make or attract one perfect for you. And look for the best coach you can afford, making sure both of you want to get to where you want. It doesn't have to be local, it can be anyone from around the world. You just need a phone, Skype, FaceTime, GoToMeeting, or Free Conference Call. The ultimate is a face-to-face with the person, and then you really see and feel their sincerity and energy! Let your heart and gut make it happen.

As my Grandfather Leigh Harline's song says, "When You Wish Upon a Star," your dreams come true.

To contact Leigh:

I'd be honored to have a free or multiple free conversations with anyone, by first emailing me. ladams00@icloud.com.

leighadamscoaching.com

LinkedIn: Leigh Adams

Home: (909) 980-3257

Cell: (909) 223-5297

Donna Dahl

Donna Dahl is a professional personal coach, self-help author and inspirational speaker. She has been described as a thought leader and a personal empowerment catalyst. If you asked Donna what motivates her to engage others, she would say, "It's the magic that happens when their personal power is ignited into action."

When Donna isn't writing a chapter for her next book or learning something new, she's working with her coaching clients or sharing her time and talents in the service of others. A highlight of her volunteer experience has been being a guest lecturer delivering a class entitled, "Innovation" to senior university students.

Donna was honored with the Queen Elizabeth II Diamond Jubilee Medal in 2012, and the 100th Anniversary International Women's Day Outstanding Service Award in business in 2011. She has a Master's Degree in Educational Psychology and is a Master Practitioner of Neuro Linguistic Programming.

She has written four inspiring books. Her blog, which could be subtitled "Life Hacks by Donna," illustrates ways in which challenges expand our experience.

Donna currently resides in Calgary, Alberta, with her husband, Ron.

Determined

By Donna Dahl

"Being deeply loved by someone gives you strength, while loving someone deeply gives you courage." - Lao Tzu

A car accident is a nasty event. One minute I was a vibrant, go-getter with energy to take on the world; the next minute I was traumatized. The loud crunch of metal crashing into metal rang in my ears.

Within 24 hours of the accident, my body felt like it had been hammered from head to toe. My muscles were stiff. It hurt to move. I was in pain. To my chagrin, I was walking with a significant limp and it took a great deal more effort to dress myself and comb my hair than I thought it should. It was the morning after "the event." To put it bluntly, I felt like hell. I would not be going to work that day. I reluctantly made the call.

I was confused. I had no broken bones. I had not so much as a scratch. I had no visible injury. The car that hit me from behind as I was stopped in traffic had, however, hit me hard enough to damage my gas tank and push my car forward into the car stopped in front of me. I braced myself for what was about to take place. I held my foot on the brake as firmly as I could to keep my car from causing injury to anyone in the car in front of me. It worked. The only one injured was me.

I estimate that my car weighed between 3000 and 4000 pounds. Maybe I should have been limping. Maybe I should have been sore. Being only five feet tall and not a pound over weight may have had something to do with how I was feeling. Surely, this condition was purely temporary.

I can't be certain but I think instinct took over when I saw the car behind me heading straight for the back of my car. Maybe it wasn't instinct; maybe it was panic. I had nowhere to turn and no time to make a move. I applied the brake and held on to that steering wheel with every ounce of muscle I had.

After the accident, I spent the next decade attempting to restore the physical and mental parts of me that I had lost. I had lost muscle strength. I had suffered loss of memory function and I had trouble concentrating. Learning new things was laborious. My ability to participate in conversation was almost non-existent. I frequently found myself stopped in the middle of a sentence not remembering what I was going to say next. I went from happy social butterfly to isolated cocoon. From a career perspective, my self-image was shattered. I could no longer work. The people I used to work with were no longer part of my day or part of my life. I had given more than 20 years of my life to my profession. That all evaporated at the point of impact. Who was I? Who was this person that couldn't even share a story? I didn't know her and I didn't much care to acknowledge her. I didn't like the way she changed. I didn't like the person she had become.

What if I couldn't change her back? What a silly question! Of course, I could change her back. There was no way that I could let words like "can't" or "fear" into my thoughts. "Can't" is for sissies. Fear is a luxury. Fear stunts effort. Fear allows time to pass without productivity.

There was no time for fear. I had to believe I could get her back. I could not picture accepting myself the way I was. The question then became, "What would I have to do to get her back?" How long would it take? How long would my family and my medical team of supporters hang in there with me? How long would my husband hold my hand?

Healing exaggerated unusual things in my mind. For example, the family telephone directory was in my brain. I used to carry all those phone numbers around in my head. Now those numbers were inaccessible. You may think this was hardly significant but it was another one of those things on an already too-long list that had developed a vacancy sign. Do I grieve for the part of me that is missing? Do I accept the vacancy sign and move on? Do I attempt to re-train my brain?

The timing of the accident could not have been worse. I had married the love of my life the year before. It felt like we were living our version of a storybook love story; we could not have been happier. Our plan was to live a long, happily-ever-after life in our new marriage. Then came this accident and all the accompanying aftermath. My independence was suddenly compromised. My social life came to a screeching halt. I felt isolated. My attentional focus to matters at hand was subject to my attentional limits, and these were out of my control. I wrote list upon list upon list to help me keep myself on track. Loving my husband was easy. Taking care of myself to heal was daunting. No, it was more than daunting. It was downright uncomfortable. I was a nurturer; I was accustomed to nurturing the needs of others before my own. I needed to prove to myself and to my husband that I was never giving up. I was going to make the journey back.

My affirmations attracted doubt. What if I was more of a danger to myself than I realized? What if I did leave a burner on the stove unattended? These "what ifs" were frightening. They made my husband afraid to leave me on my own. He found himself making the time to take me to medical appointments when I was terrified to drive. I could not dispel the anxiety that someone might rear-end me again.

I worked hard at healing. I walked a mile a day or more. No matter how much I walked, I could not pick up the speed. Improvement stalled out in less than a month. I kept walking. I attended physiotherapy sessions. I received acupuncture. I did what I could to the best of my ability.

All the appointments, the various therapies, the tests and the treatments took their toll on us separately and individually. We were getting discouraged. Fatigue began to set in. We would rather have been dancing than arranging my husband's schedule to match the next visit to the doctor. We were growing tired of the outlay of the time and energy we were devoting to my recovery. The investments seemed to far outweigh the benefits. My progress toward a satisfactory outcome was minimal at best. Anger crept in. Hope was diminishing.

What kept us both together started with love. It was from that foundation that we both believed there was a way back from this dark and pessimistic place. We both believed that my return to vitality was possible. But we needed to move beyond hope.

I needed a soft place to land. My husband's solution was to remove me from the environment that reminded me day-to-day of my losses and the role I formerly played in my community. It had become increasingly more difficult emotionally for us to be around people who remembered me as inspiring and capable but who came to see me as unengaged and dysfunctional. The longer I stayed around my "before" life, the worse I felt about myself and the angrier I got.

I needed an advocate who was on my side 100 per cent of the way. To solve this, my husband took on the role of being my project manager. He began by connecting me with as many compassionate helpers as he could find and he even attended appointments with me. He took the approach that I needed a vocal supporter if I was to heal. His intercessions were, indeed, a source of strength. I no longer felt like I was alone. My conviction to heal grew exponentially.

Days turned into months. Months turned into years. Years passed. My lack of improvement was increasingly testing our resolve. Medications prescribed for pain challenged the long-term health of my body. Time spent in physical therapies often turned out to feel more palliative than productive. Gains, if any, were short-lived. My patience was wearing thin.

I believed I knew what was missing in my treatment program. I wanted help with my expressive speech. I wanted help with my memory. I wanted help with regaining my ability to demonstrate balance. I wanted help with muscle development. None of these were made available to me and taking any steps in that direction without my physician's consent would label me as a non-compliant patient.

If I was to stand a chance of returning to my former self, my husband and I felt there was only one option for me. I needed to be free of the caregivers that weren't matching my expectation for delivering positive change. By the time 10 years from the accident had passed, the umbilical cord binding me to long-term disability status was severed. I was pursuing a self-managed, multi-disciplinary approach to healing and my husband and I started to re-connect as a couple.

I knew what I wanted. No one was ever going to give me back my years of lost career time or my ten years of lost romance in a new marriage. And no one was going to stand in my way to make the most of the rest of my life. I gathered in my mind the things that I thought were missing from my treatment regime and I wrote them down in the form of wishes. Things started to change.

I had started to learn Tai Chi before the accident. Perhaps this could serve me. So I signed up for classes at a level I thought I could handle. I quickly discovered that I couldn't follow the instructor. Face-on instructions turned into "gobbledy-goo" in my brain. I frequently found myself on the wrong foot or facing the wrong direction and falling behind. Sometimes the exercises required me to balance on one foot. I had to cheat. A balance pose for me was standing on one foot while my big toe from my other foot grounded me to the floor. I often arrived home with a headache. I liked being involved in an activity that didn't require conversation. But after two years of classes, I wondered if I was ever going to get my sense of balance back. I put Tai Chi on hold. Another disappointment.

I bought a bicycle. I hoped the skills of balance I had learned riding a two-wheeler as a child would still be available to me. They were. That was the first positive starting point I had had in years. I knew I turned a corner.

Wearing sleeveless garments revealed that my right arm looked like a stick compared to my left and I'm right handed. I refused to accept the diagnosis that the muscle in my arm was "spent." I found myself watching the movie, "The Karate Kid," where the young protégé was asked by the master to perform a muscle-building activity called "wax on, wax off." The magic of the activity grew with each repetition. There were many activities within the realm of keeping house wherein I could apply "wax on, wax off." I started with the bathtub. In the beginning I worked with a small patch about the size of a face cloth. It took a couple of weeks to work the entire tub using this method but I persisted. If I could practice the Karate Kid technique on the bath tub, I could graduate from waxing the hardwood floor to painting the deck. It took two weeks to paint 150 square feet of deck that first time. I didn't care how long it took. The important part for me was empowering my arm. Within six months, I could clench my fist and make a muscle. I started to see a difference. "Wax on, wax off" was working for me.

One day out of the blue, a licensed elocutionist showed up in my life. The timing of her appearance ranks up there with words like, "wow" - not any ordinary wow, but a "wow" that felt huge in an over-the-top sort of way. Imagine reading "WOW" in bold letters as tall as this page. That was the size of the overwhelming feeling that came over me.

She asked if she could take me on as a client. I wanted to cry. Could she have read my wish list? I agreed to accept her as my speaking coach and I immediately began attending appointments. What a blessing! With her immense knowledge of the anatomy of speech, she took me from hesitant and halting phrases where words got lost in my vocabulary closet to being able to express myself without fear or evidence of disability.

As a former student of Huna, traditions based in Hawaiian culture, I had learned that "energy flows where attention goes." Looking back at my three wishes and the experiences that followed, I now see how I made a conscious effort to direct my attention to these three focal points of healing. I also now understand the power in Lao Tzu's words that love magnifies the influence of conviction. I know my husband's love was key to my recovery.

My journey through change was anything but comfortable. Change is part of life. Sometimes change can be predicted, mapped and produced according to a logistical plan. Sometimes change simply arrives without notice. Then what?

What about uninvited change and the effect it might be having on your life? Change can be instantaneous and unexpected. It can be welcome or unwelcome. Change can be anticipated as with expecting a baby. It can be chaotic. Change can be so wrapped up in chaos that it results in incapacitating confusion. As well, change can be a stimulus: it can be the bearer of hope and it can be a remarkable event separating your past from your future.

Do you believe that change is an opportunity to achieve something better than what was present before? Do you believe in yourself? Do you believe in your talents and abilities to weather storms or manifest dreams?

Do you believe that the solutions for personal repair or reconstruction motivated by change can introduce you to teachers and guides to assist your progress? Do you believe you are worthy of personal instruction and suitable recognition for your accomplishments?

I could not have worked through the change back to health without an entire cadre of care-givers and helpers. While I have not changed completely back to the person I was, I feel new and improved in many ways - physically, emotionally, and spiritually. And I learned a lot.

I learned that I was still lovable despite my shortcomings. I learned that I could accept the new me with the added flaws attached. I learned that I could love the woman who was injured on that fateful September day and that I could forgive her for having been in harm's way.

I learned a system for making my wishes come true. I *identified* my wishes, *isolated* them from all the rest of the debilitating clutter that was dragging me toward despair and gave them *priority space* in my life by committing them to a list that I wrote down.

I learned that there are "angels" among us who are ready to step up and join our journey. While I now have a much stronger appreciation for making wishes and allowing them to be manifested, I also know what it means to attract helpers and work as a team to manifest dreams. In fact, if it weren't for accepting an invitation from a successful local publisher to write articles for one of her magazines, I may not ever have turned that page and begun to write professionally.

I learned that I needed to be open to the appearance of these "angels," mentors, and significant others in order to receive their gifts for healing. I learned that I not only needed to acknowledge them but that I also needed to engage them.

There is not a day goes by when I do not deliberately and wholeheartedly express my gratitude for all those who took the time to show up in my life when I needed them. They coached me to re-ignite some of the dormant spaces in my brain. They supported me to re-awaken physical skills even though I was coming from a position of deficit. They shared their wisdom. They believed in me.

Collectively and individually, my angels contributed to the success of my journey through the physically debilitating leftovers from the accident. I am now able to once again participate in life in high gear. For this I am truly and eternally grateful. My gratitude does not stop there. My angels continue to show up in ways that sometimes bring tears to my eyes. They surprise me. They humble me.

A dear friend calls me fearless. Does fearlessness show up without an invitation?

It's easy to ask people with limitations to accept the lemons before them and get on with making the lemonade. It's quite another thing to be determined to paint the lemons orange and discover the resources to make it happen. Change is a choice. Change powered by love, supported by helpers, and fueled by determination can create profound results.

To contact Donna:

www.donnadahl.ca

www.twitter.com/DonnaDahl

www.linkedin.com/pub/dir/Donna/Dahl

Visit her blog and her website at www.donnadahl.ca

M Marzuki Mohamed

M Marzuki Mohamed has extensive experience in the field of Human Capital Development. Not only is he an excellent, dynamic and resourceful instructor of international standing, he is also skilled in the management and leadership of an organization with international experience in the field of construction. His success in management and leadership stems from his starting premise that every person is an individual human being and a special entity that makes a difference in this world. Thus, it is with this principle that he ventured into training and teaching to generate widespread and effective impact to this message.

Participants to his programs receive enhanced benefits and more impact full results from his training and coaching because of his extensive practical knowledge and skillful application of Neuro and Behavioral Sciences using the Accelerated Learning technology.

Marzuki is a Certified Neuro-Semantics and NLP Trainer, and Associate Certified Meta-Coach by the International Society of Neuro-Semantics®.

Grow Or Die!

By M Marzuki Mohamed

The specialist construction company that I grew for six years died the day I left it in 1998.

No, the company didn't actually die but the specialist construction company died. I was the expert in the company. When I left, I left with the company's expertise. It had to turn into general construction, as its expertise was gone.

BUILDING EXPERTISE

After graduating as a civil engineer in 1985, I joined a start-up construction company, specializing in soil improvement. As the design engineer, I had to quickly learn the technical specialization of the company. At the time, it specialized in a soil improvement technology using vertical drainage. I had a senior in the company, a co-engineer who appeared to me to be at the forefront of technology. I used to look over his shoulder at what he was working on, the books that he read and followed him to the conferences on the latest developments in soil improvement technology. Starting off with Vertical Drainage, we helped the company develop additional specialist techniques in soil improvement technology, such as Vibro-Compaction, Dynamic Compaction, Stone Columns and other soil reinforcement and stabilization techniques.

Within five years, we became subject matter experts in Malaysia. Developers came to us for advice on their projects on marginal lands. Consulting engineers consulted us on the most appropriate engineering solution to improve the ground for their projects. Contractors engaged us for the most cost-effective soil improvement solution. Universities and regulatory bodies invited us to give talks and seminars. The technologies that we imported from other experts from the Netherlands, Germany, Hong Kong and Japan, we were now exporting to Singapore, Indonesia, Brunei, Thailand and Vietnam. We were respected in the field of soil improvement and business was good.

How do you get to be an expert? You deliberately work on it, one skill at a time to gain competency. Then you need to deliberately develop your competency, one element at a time, to gain expertise.

The oft-repeated phrase is practice makes perfect. No! Practice makes permanent! Deliberate practice makes perfect. That is why you need to deliberately practice your skills in order to gain expertise.

COMPETENCY = ATTITUDE + SKILL + KNOWLEDGE

Your attitude about learning is key. How do you think-feel about learning? Do you feel good about it? Are you enthusiastic about learning? Are you curious to learn? If you answered "Yes!" to these questions, then 80% of the problem is solved. Do you realize that 95% of the people do NOT read non-fiction books after they graduate from high school, college or university? No wonder that only 5% of the people consider themselves to be successful in life. You need to have a learner's mind-set, a BEGINNER'S MIND. The beginner's mind is like the mind of a child. It is ever curious, ever probing and asking questions. Do you remember the questions you asked as a child? Do you remember the questions you were asked by a child? I remember a question my daughter asked me when she was about four. "Daddy, why is fire hot?" I opened my mouth to provide a glib answer, took a deep breath and shut it again because I realized that I didn't know the real answer! Luckily for us, I had the honesty to reply, "Fia, daddy doesn't know the answer to that question. Why don't we look for the answer together?" By admitting that I did not know, I accidentally activated my beginner's mind. A year later, as I was reading *Critical Path* by Richard Buckminster Fuller, the answer to that question jumped out of its pages and I was able to share that with her.

The Beginner's Mind is all about attitude towards learning. Having the right attitude about learning will spur you to acquire more and more knowledge. LEARNING IS THE KEY FOR GROWTH. Without learning, stagnation sets in, then regression and ultimately death.

Learning is a skill that can be learned; that has to be learned. When you have the skills of learning, then you are opening yourself up to Word Lessons and World Lessons.

Word Lessons are the lessons that you learn from reading books, listening to audio lessons, viewing video lessons and attending classes, seminars or training. Now, which of these are you doing right now?

Then there are the World Lessons. These are the events that you go through in life and each event is there for learning for you. One major skill that will stand by you for World Lessons is the skill of self-reflection. To reflect upon each event and asking yourself, "What do I learn from this?"

You may begin by developing technical excellence in the field that you are currently in. Having the commitment to excellence in that particular field to become an expert in it. Robert Pante, master life coach and author of *Image Builds Business,* and other books, puts out a challenge that I find most compelling when he defined excellence. "On your worst day, you are better than anyone else on their best day." What are you good at? What field are you currently in? What field can you master? What skills do you need to enhance to become a master in your field?

Other than excellence in your chosen technical area, you may also begin developing other transferable skills. For me, at the top of the list is the leadership set of skills. What are they? What does a leader need to do? A leader creates an inspiring vision of the future. A leader engages people with that vision such that the people identify themselves with the vision. A leader then manages the accomplishment of the vision. A leader builds and coaches teams to actualize the vision. Leadership brings together all the skills necessary to do all of these. To learn these, start by understanding the systems and processes in your organization - systems thinking. Then, for you to appreciate the systemic nature of how each component in the organization affect other components - systemic thinking.

ENTREPRENEURIAL MINDSET

In 1987 the country and the region went through an economic downtown. The construction industry was first hit. Construction projects began grinding to a halt. Payment for work done, slowed down. Aging list began to lengthen; payment that was supposed to be made in 30-days, dragged to 60-days, then to 90-days, then to 120-days. Companies struggled to make salary payments. I remember working for two months without pay and then receive half a month's salary. What did we do? Apart from doing what we can do to reduce cost for the company, like using our private vehicles to transport equipment to project sites, we kept a close relationship with the client's chain of command from the project manager right up to the finance manager. By doing that, whenever the client has money to disburse, our company would be included. In that way, we kept our salaries from drying-up altogether.

Some may be tempted to say that payment of salaries is the responsibility of the company owner. Well, we started thinking like the company owner to make sure that the company has money to pay our salaries. We could have just said, "I have done my job. It's the boss' job to pay me my salary!" No! We began thinking, "Where can I collect money for the company so that it can pay us our salaries?" We began thinking like the entrepreneur and taking responsibility for our own situations instead of leaving it to others.

Thinking like an entrepreneur, instead of employee mind-set, and thinking about responsibilities, instead of entitlement mind-set, are critical if you want to survive and thrive in times of accelerating change. You cannot rely on others to make things better for you. You cannot rely on your current competencies and to keep doing what you have always been doing. You need to ask yourself, "What do they want? How do I give that to them?" 'They' and 'them' here refer to your customers - your boss, your company, the company's customers, vendors and stakeholders. What is the 'value' that you need to give to them? What additional competencies do I need to be able to do that? If you keep on thinking, "I am the <profession> here and this is what I do," then you will very swiftly be as dead as the dodo.

CHANGE

By 1990, the economy had picked up considerably and the company was doing very well. So well that the company began to expand into infrastructure engineering, building construction, environmental engineering and even information technology. Geotechnical engineering, which was the sole source of income for the company before the additional businesses, then became a small department and contributor to the company's coffers. The pioneers and the stalwarts of the company were happy for the company's success until words that resulted in ill feelings began to filter into our ears. Words like, "What are these engineers doing, playing with their computers all-day long?" Many felt unappreciated. After all the hard work and sacrifices to sustain the company while it was in dire need, and the bosses had this to say when things turned for the better. People began to leave.

Eighty percent of people leave the company they worked in because of their bosses. There are competent bosses and there are less than competent bosses. How do less than competent bosses come about? One of the reasons how less than competent bosses come about in many corporate and public organizations is that people get promoted to positions of their incompetency. Let say that you are an engineer and you are very good in your particular area of engineering expertise. After years of solid work to the organization, the company decided to promote you to engineering manager. You have now been promoted to a position of your incompetency. Engineering competency and management competency require different skill sets. Whereas in engineering, you mainly concern yourself with the 3 M's; Materials, Machines and Methods, in management you need to concern yourself with the fourth M; that is Man. You need people skills apart from technical skill. What happens to many bosses is that when they get promoted to their position of incompetency, they revert to their areas of competency. That is why you may find that many engineering managers revert back to doing the work of engineers rather than managing their engineers.

Many people want to feel appreciated in the jobs that they do. When they end up with a boss who does not know how to manage people, they feel unappreciated and unhappy. So, what do you do if you have such a boss? This is one of the most often asked questions amongst executives and non-executives when I run my training programs.

Even amongst managers, they would ask this same question about their bosses!

First thing to remember is you cannot change others. You can only change yourself. "For things to change first I must change." Yes, it feels good when people appreciate you. At the same time, do not expect appreciation from others. When you are not expecting it and they do, it feels good.

If they don't, it doesn't really matter, does it? What is more important is that you know how to appreciate yourself. Do you know how to appreciate yourself? How do you know that you have done a good job? This leads us to the second point - know how to measure your performance.

In the industrial age, the measure of performance is time. In the information age, the measure of performance is result. Thus, performance measurement is as equally important a skill as performing the job itself. There are lead measures and lag measures as well as tangible measures and intangible measures. Do you know how to measure all of them?

Lag indicators are measures focusing on results at the end of a time period, normally characterizing historical performance. Market share, sales, employee satisfaction are examples of lag indicators. They are normally easy to identify and capture. They are historical in nature and do not reflect current activities and lack predictive power.

Lead indicators, on the other hand, are measures that drive or lead to the performance of lag measures, normally measuring intermediate processes and activities. Hours spent with customers, proposals written, absenteeism are examples of lead indicators. They are predictive in nature and allow organizations to make adjustments to achieve desired results. Lead indicators may prove difficult to identify and capture, and often new measures with no history in the organization.

Measures that are tangible in nature, such as net income, market share, output per production and absenteeism, are easier to capture. When measures are intangible, such as innovativeness, continuous learning, quality, commitment and customer focus, they may be more subjective in nature and more difficult to capture.

You may ask, "Why bother to measure my own performance? Is that not what the boss is supposed to do every year end?" Yes, the boss is tasked with appraising your performance. The question is, "How well is he be able to measure your performance?" Does he stand guard over you all the time when you are at work? Is that all that he is tasked to do or is he not also tasked to do his own job? Is he also not being measured for doing his own job? If he is, which he definitely is, then would he not be more concerned about measuring his performance than measuring yours? Does it not make more sense for you to measure your own performance so that you have evidence of the quality of your performance? Measuring your own performance is your responsibility. If you do not know how to measure your own performance, do not expect your boss to know how to either. And be ready to be under-evaluated and disappointed with your performance appraisal.

RE-ENGINEERING

I felt under-appreciated and unjustly evaluated by my bosses at the time. I, too, decided to leave but not after key technical people had left en masse. That was when I was hit with a bigger issue. I became indispensable to the company and I couldn't leave. I was threatened with, "If you leave the company, we'll close down the whole department and we'll have to fire everyone there." I was naive enough to fall for the trick and stayed, but not after getting them to agree to incorporate the department and that I would run the new company. I resolved that the livelihood of people in a company should not be held ransom by an individual and that people should be appreciated for the good work that they do.

"What do I know about management of an organization?" That was the first question I asked myself and the answer was, "Very little!" So, I started with what I knew: engineering and systems. Thus I began to systemize work processes. The area that I particularly looked into was information management for efficient storage and retrieval of information. That was the easy part.

I was most aware of my lack of experience in financial and organizational management. I had to learn that, very quickly. I attended courses and seminars to up-skill myself in these areas. Whatever that I learned, I immediately applied to running the company. I hired experienced people in areas that I lacked experience. The company grew and grew - from a turnover of $250,000 to $40,000,000 in six years. I was happy and the people were happy. However, there was one thing that was still nagging me. I was the CEO and I was still the technical expert of the company. I had two engineers that I was grooming to take over my place but I was not doing a good job of it. At the time, I did not know how to train them and I did not know why I was failing.

"The livelihood of people in a company should not be held ransom by an individual," and I was still that individual. Then, I did not even know that there was terminology for the issue that I was facing - knowledge management. In as much as I was growing through continuous learning, beginning with specialized technical knowledge in soil mechanics and soil improvement, I turned to learning about project management, business management, financial management, organizational management and performance management. The company, from the perspective of technical expertise, was not. Though I was able to transfer much of my management knowledge into organizational processes, I failed in developing new experts and translating the expertise into system processes in the company. Looking back, I now see why I was failing to do so. It was leadership. More specifically two core sub-skills of leadership and they are communicating and coaching.

Communicating is more than just speaking. It involves listening, supporting and questioning. Without these three sub-skills, I was merely talking and telling. I may be enthused about technical expertise but I know next to nothing about what was going through peoples' minds. What were their hopes and desires? What was it that they want and what drives them? What was stopping them from achieving their dreams? Was it fear, doubt, confidence, self-esteem or what?

I was trying to drive them towards a goal that I wanted using the way that I used!

Coaching skills would have allowed me to elicit their private goals and link these to the organizational goal. It would have helped them to identify their stumbling blocks and utilize their internal resources to overcome these. It would have helped them to elicit their success strategies and use them in achieving their goals in ways that work for them.

GROW OR DIE!

The company's score card was not balanced. The company was healthy from the customer, internal business process and financial perspectives. From the technical expertise standpoint, there was very little learning and growth of the organization.

Growth is mandatory. You need to grow to develop. You need to grow to be empowered. Growth is part of change.

When I approached a second roadblock in my career, and this time I decided to leave, I left with the company's expertise. The specialist construction company that I grew for six years died that day. Grow or Die!

To contact M Marzuki Mohamed:

A.L. Advancement of Human Potential Sdn Bhd

marzuki@born2excel.com

http://www.marzukimohamed.com

Pamela Wigglesworth

Results. They're what every business strives for - be in an increase in sales, generating more leads and customers or perhaps improving brand awareness in the marketplace. International corporate trainer, speaker and Managing Director of Experiential Hands-on Learning, Pamela Wigglesworth is passionate about helping SMEs and entrepreneurs shorten their learning curve and accelerate their business results.

She is the author of *Public Relations*; *Small Business Acceleration: Get Noticed using Facebook, LinkedIn, Email Marketing, Public Relations and Video Marketing* and is a co-author in book 4 of *The Change* book series.

Pamela works with companies across multiple industries to enhance their branding, marketing communications to get big results on a small budget. In addition, she assists corporate clients with sales presentation skills and coaches on advanced presentation performance. She has trained and spoken in Singapore, Malaysia, China, Indonesia, Brunei, Cambodia, Thailand and the Philippines.

She is a professional member of the Asia Professional Speakers – Singapore and served as the 2011-2012 Vice President. Pamela is a frequent speaker at business events and has several articles published in the Straits Times and Singapore Marketer magazine. She has resided in Asia for over 25 years.

Go For It! Follow Your Bliss

By Pamela Wigglesworth

As you read the above title, some of you might be saying, "Follow my what? How can I go for it when I don't know what "it" is or what bliss is?" Well, thank you for asking. Before I answer, let me ask you this question:

What would your life be like if you made the conscious decision early in your career to do what you really love; to follow your bliss? Think about that for a moment.

Over the years when I speak to students and adults alike, no matter where in the world I am, the story is the same. Young people are encouraged to go into a career that pays well… to become a doctor, lawyer, architect, engineer, or the like. They are advised to get a "real job" and forego the dream of doing what they truly love or are passionate about.

So when I say, "Follow your bliss," what does that mean? Bliss is an emotional state that is characterized by perfect happiness, that is, feelings of enjoyment, pleasure, and satisfaction. Making the decision to follow your bliss is the first step. Declare what you want, and then go for it.

I want to share with you a few lessons from my life that I hope will get you on the path and keep you on the road to your bliss. I'm going to share with you the good, the bad, and the ugly with the aim of shortening your learning curve to achieving your bliss. Let's start with the first lesson.

Listen To Your Heart

When I got out of high school (we were living in Dublin, California, at the time), I went to college at California State University, East Bay, to study biochemistry. I found the sciences interesting and thought I wanted to do cancer research. I was down to the third quarter of the fourth year of my studies, and we were taking final exams.

I was taking the exam for a physical chemistry course, or P-chem as the students called it. As I sat in my seat, I started to scroll down the test paper to review the questions. I read the first one and thought, "Hmm…, I don't know that one." Got to the second one: "Don't know that one either." I continued down the paper and realized that I didn't know any of the answers.

Then it struck me like someone hitting me on the head with a brick. I didn't know any of the answers because I really wasn't interested in the subject. I realized then and there that doing research for the rest of my life was not what I wanted to do. I surmised that I had gone into the sciences because it was a subject that my dad would be happy I pursued.

I think I knew all along that my passion and desire was in the world of fashion, but I was told I wouldn't be able to earn a decent living, that I wasn't going to be the next Donna Karen or Coco Chanel, and so I'd better pursue a "real" job.

So as I sat there looking at the exam paper, I thought, "I have two options. I can sit here and doodle on my exam paper for the next two hours, or I can get up and turn my paper in to the professor." Twenty minutes into the exam, I chose the latter. As I walked toward the front of the room, I could hear the gasps from the other students. They were probably thinking, "She's either a genius, or something is terribly wrong." I thanked the professor for his time and told him that science was not for me, wished him all the best, and left the classroom.

That evening I told my parents that I had walked out and that it was the end of my science career. Of course they thought I was nuts at the time and I found out later from friends that they wondered if I was having a nervous breakdown.

Following my departure from the exam, I continued to work at my full time job until once again, it came to me that what I really wanted all along was to study fashion design. I understood that I needed to listen to my heart and do what I loved. Eighteen months later, I enrolled in the Fashion Institute of Design and Merchandising (FIDM) in San Francisco. Walking out of my physical chemistry exam was the pivotal point for my entire career. It started the chain of events that led to my enrollment in design school. It put me on the path to finding my bliss.

Do Whatever It Takes

I was thrilled to be accepted into FIDM, yet the tuition was quite high. Rather than start immediately, I asked to wait until the next intake so I could save money for the tuition, apply for a student loan, and look for any available grants and scholarships.

The student loan came through, but no grant or scholarship. During that time my brother-in-law was managing a fast food hamburger restaurant and he gave me a part-time job. It was a bit embarrassing to have my high school and college friends come into the place and see me in uniform proclaiming, "Welcome to Jack in the Box. May I take your order?" But the need for extra money far outweighed my momentary embarrassment. So embarrassing or not, you must do whatever it takes to follow your bliss.

By working the evening shift from 6:00 p.m. to midnight, and working my union wage job at a grocery chain during the day, I managed to save enough for my tuition. Back then, fashion design students did their second year of classes in Los Angeles. Because I didn't want to have to work my second year of school I continued working both jobs while going to school the first year, and put away enough for a nice little nest egg.

Midway through my first year of school, my family was hit with a major financial crisis, and we lost the family home. I spent my nest egg to get the family moved into a new place. Keeping the family together just meant I'd have to continue to work and go to school.

At the time of the crisis, my mother was quite upset and I remember her asking me, "The money you just gave us, that was your school money, wasn't it?" I told her yes. She said, "I guess that means you won't be able to go to school in Los Angeles next year." I told her, "I'm going. I don't care if I have to work a third job. I'm going." I then squeezed in sewing, mother-of-the-bride dresses as my third job. Following your bliss means that you'll do whatever it takes.

I mentioned earlier that I had applied for a variety of grants and scholarships. When it came to reviewing the tuition for the second year of school, I requested a meeting with the Dean. He looked at my list of 40 companies and organizations where I had applied for scholarships, and at the pile of rejection letters that lay before him on his desk.

After looking at my college transcripts and the letters before him, he said, "Clearly you wanted to come to our design college. You made a great effort to seek financial aid, but were not able to secure any assistance. Any person who makes that kind of effort to come to our school, I know will become a wonderful student. As the Dean of this college, I have the authority to make exceptions with the tuition and therefore I am reducing the second year tuition by one-third."

He could see that I was willing to do whatever it took to follow my bliss. You too must also do whatever it takes to follow your bliss.

Surround Yourself With Positive People

As you move forward in your career, whatever industry you venture into, it is important to surround yourself with positive people. In a challenging economy, you're going to find a lot of unhappy and frustrated people. They will moan and groan about how tough it is out there. Trust me, this does not have to be your reality.

Despite all the doom and gloom that you read and hear about in the news, a downturn in the economy does not have to affect your reality. Not only can you survive in such an environment, you can thrive. During the years when the economy has been sluggish I've managed to increase the turnover in my business and create new opportunities for myself. Such accomplishments can come about only when you are surrounded by like-minded people. I call these people my support buddies, my cheerleaders. They are the ones who won't let you mope around or have a pity party. They are the ones who will kick you in the shins if you need it or lend a helping hand or a listening ear.

Be mindful of the people you hang out with. The inspirational motivational speaker, the late Jim Rohn said, "You are the average of the five people you spend the most time with." Think about that for a moment. If you are looking to become a high net worth individual, then you need to hang out with other high net worth people.

Start a mastermind group of four to six people. Meet every two weeks or once a month to bounce your ideas off of one another. I belong to a speaker/trainer mastermind group and have another support buddy in Europe that I Skype with regularly.

Look around you. Who do you know who will make a great cheerleader or would be great to have in a mastermind group? If you can't find someone within your immediate circle of friends (which is sometimes the case), then consider finding a group of like-minded people online. Look within business organizations for people who will support you and help move you forward. Be Authentic, Be Yourself

It is so important that you be authentic, be yourself. Be who you are and not what other people want you to be or who you think the world wants you to be.

As the daughter of an Army officer, I had the privilege of living overseas in Germany and Indonesia. When my family returned to the US, my parents purchased a house in California. It was going to take some time to get all the documentation finalized so we moved in with my aunt for three months. She lived in St. Louis, Missouri, in a ghetto neighborhood made up predominately of low income black families.

On the first day of school as I was registering for classes (I was in junior high), I expressed to the administrator that I would like to take Spanish as my foreign language elective. She looked at me and said, "What?" I repeated myself and explained that I wanted to take Spanish. She turned to her colleague behind the counter, burst out laughing, and said, "Mildred, did you hear that? She wants to take Spanish!" She turned to me and said, "Spanish, you want to take Spanish? Honey, these kids here can't even speak English, and you want to take Spanish!" She kept laughing under her breath and repeating, "She wants to take Spanish!"

Later that day I had my first class, which was an English class. The teacher gave instructions for the exercise, which was for the first student to make a statement. The second student in the row had to repeat the statement and add onto it. It went down the row like that with everyone repeating the sentence and adding their bit, yet all in Black English (Ebonics).

Unfortunately, I wasn't able to speak in the vernacular, so when it was my turn to share, I used the grammar, tense, and intonation of standard English. I never made it through the entire sentence because the whole class was roaring with laughter. When I asked the teacher if there was something I did wrong, she told me that they were laughing at my "good" English.

Those three months of school were horrific for my siblings and me. We were social outcasts. We were told that we talked like white people, that we were Oreos, black on the outside, but white on the inside. I remember making a decision early on that I would do everything in my power to carry myself in such a way that no one would ever judge me as an ignorant black woman.

What I learned from that experience carried on into my corporate life and my speaking career. When I became a business owner, I always wore a suit or a dress and very rarely dress slacks. I made sure that I dotted my i's and crossed my t's so that people would see me as an upstanding, intelligent black woman.

I operated that way for the longest time, until one day just before giving a lunch-time talk to a group of bank executives, I decided to drop the "proper" façade and let the audience see the fun and crazy, yet professional Pamela. We had a fun 90 minutes together and when I was done, I knew it was the best talk I had ever given. I knew I was in "the zone" and the audience felt it too. One executive shared that he had been attending lunch time talks with the bank for 10 years and that my talk was the best he had heard.

The talk was a huge success because the audience got to see me. I was authentic; I was myself. I've operated that way ever since. Be authentic. People can spot when you are not being sincere. Remove any mask that hides you and give others the best of you.

Fail Forward

Over the 25 years of my entrepreneurial career, I have started four companies. The second company was a line of women's clothing that was sold within my own boutique in Singapore.

My clientele consisted of locals, tourists, and predominantly expat women, or put another way, full figure gals with hips and busts like mine, who had difficulty finding clothing in their size. As the business grew, we moved from a second story shophouse to a downtown shopping center, where our overheads were about $15,000 a month.

In late 1998, shortly before we relocated, Asia was struck by the first financial crisis. We didn't see an immediate effect, but over time, the business started to feel the impact of the slowing economy. Overall people were shopping less; many only spent on necessities. People started to lose their jobs, and expats were being repatriated. Fewer and fewer women shopped in my store. The business was bleeding. The shopping center became quieter and quieter.

Then one day I received the sales figures from my store manager. I knew right then and there that the business was dying and we weren't going to make it. I knew I would have to say goodbye to the staff, people dear to me, and close the store.

When it came to dealing with the landlords, I had hoped that they would be sympathetic to my plight and allow me to gracefully get out of my lease, but that was really wishful thinking. They knocked off two weeks and I had to pay the landlord the balance: $42,000.

That money came from my husband's and my savings. As much as we hated to write that check, we knew that we had to do it then or things could become worse down the road.

When I looked at what I could have done differently, I realized that I needed to have done more marketing, an area that I had little understanding or expertise in at the time.

So after closing the shop, I took some time to reflect. In doing so, I realized that I had a failed business, not that I had personally failed. I think it is important that you understand the difference. I made the decision that I would not fall on my face and stay down on the ground having a pity party (at least not a permanent one).

Instead, I chose to fail forward. I knew the day would come when I would start another business. With the pity party over, I made the commitment to learn as much as I could about branding and marketing a small business. I wanted to make that $40,000 loss count for something. And learn I did. The experience became the catalyst that ignited a new passion - helping other companies with branding and marketing communication so they can succeed and hopefully avoid huge financial losses.

Winston Churchill once said, "Success is the ability to fail again and again and again without the loss of enthusiasm."

Don't be afraid to try something out of fear that you may fail. Failure is nothing more than a lesson in what NOT to do the next time around. Failure is a stepping stone to your success. Choose to fail forward.

The way I've dealt with the events in my life has led me to where I am today: an international speaker and coach, a marketing specialist, and author. I have the honor of working with small and medium enterprises, entrepreneurs, and multinational corporations, teaching them strategies and techniques to create an offline and online presence, increase consumer awareness, and ultimately increase their sales.

Whether it is delivering a keynote address or facilitating an SME Marketing Bootcamp, one thing is for sure: I'm following and living my bliss.

So as you begin to follow your bliss, remember to listen to your heart and do whatever it takes to follow it. Surround yourself with positive people, find those cheerleaders, those support buddies. Be authentic. Be yourself. There is no one else on the planet like you. If you encounter difficulties, remember to fail forward into your bliss.

To contact Pamela:

Tel: +(65) 6241 9834

Email: courses@experiential.sg

URL: http://www.experiential.sg

Linkedin.com/in/pamelawigglesworth

Twitter.com/ExpPam

Darcee McJannet

Darcee McJannet, is the CEO and founder of Stratego Consulting International Inc.

The World's Top Work/Life Rebalance Expert, her focus as a "Transitional Strategist" combines executive, leadership and life coaching. Mentored by the world renowned leadership guru, John C. Maxwell, she is a certified John Maxwell Team Coach. She is also an author, speaker, forward thinker and thought leader. As a visionary, she integrates personal and professional leadership development to achieve optimal life management and performance; successfully rebalancing her own life as a busy, entrepreneur, wife and mother of two.

Darcee provides opinions and commentary to the media, she has been featured in the "Game Changer" coaching movie, radio and film appearances. She writes articles for various publications and has an upcoming book on work/life rebalance.

She provides strategic coaching and consultative services in personal and professional life management, organizational restructuring/development, strategic/succession planning, change management, human capital management and employee development.

She holds a business degree and wrote a dissertation on corporate wellness. She has over 20 years of experience in various facets of leadership development, human resources, regional management, business development, client relationship management, recruitment/retention and training. As a regional manager, she successfully led cross-functional teams, effectively managing IBM'S Western Canadian operations.

Effective Work & Life ReBalance Personal & Professional Life Management

By Darcee McJannet

Modern day life is full of competing priorities, from kids to school, medical appointments, friendships, work, errands, family, and a never ending barrage of daily demands. 58% of individuals report "overload" as a result of the pressures associated with work, home and family, friends, physical health, volunteer and community service.[1] Individuals are searching for a roadmap and compass that will effectively guide them through these challenges while striving to mitigate personal stressors and anxiety that impact the body, mind, and soul. The same reality exists for all of us. We are all battling against an onslaught of competing demands with limited resources and a finite amount of time. Essentially, with only 24 hours/day, we are all resource deprived and "time poor." The world has changed, demanding new approaches.

Does work/life balance actually exist? The simple answer to the question is, no. I will start by debunking the myth and misconception that the entire notion of work/life balance is a reality. When we discuss work/life balance, there appears to be a notion that there is a proper balance that can be achieved between work and personal

---

[1] Canadian Mental Health Association

activities that will result in greater personal happiness. However, it is my belief that a healthy body, mind, and soul is a byproduct of each individual, recognizing that it is the entire entity of the person that is challenged by the competing demands, be it in their workplace or personal, life. Frankly, the 21st century is chaotic.

To effectively and efficiently manage the chaos of competing priorities, an individual must identify his/her inherent coping strategies and establish techniques that will enhance productivity and reduce barriers. How do we incorporate balance in our lives to achieve personal wealth and happiness? Our fast-paced new reality no longer allows for true balance. Instead, individuals are now forced to *"rebalance."*

Rebalancing is a conscious strategy, whereby individuals effectively ride the ebbs and flows of their physical and mental energy to optimize results during peak periods of focus, recharging when their resolve and commitment is at lower levels. *Rebalance is a proactive lifestyle philosophy and paradigm that takes control of your existence* by establishing a hierarchy prioritized by mandatory objectives, optional goals, and internal resources (time, energy, health, etc.). When you take control of your life, you begin to chart a path and a course of action.

The very essence of rebalance is to create a zone in which you can function at your optimal ability. Finding your equilibrium and optimal performance hot spot allows you to perform your best. This *rebalanced hot spot* translates into increased confidence, opportunities and internal stamina. It is imperative that you establish a rebalanced strategy, utilizing time optimization tools and techniques to have work/life prioritization. *"Achieving a rebalance involves getting into your equilibrium and optimal performance zone."*

- Darcee McJannet

Approaching life *unconsciously,* living with no sense of direction or purpose is a recipe for *unbalanced dissatisfaction,* resulting in anxiety, stress disorders, depression, hopelessness and a general feeling of malaise. In order to get your desired results, you must devise a *conscious strategic life plan and vision to enact it. Once centered in a state of rebalanced alignment, your world takes on a life of its own, filled with passion and purpose.* Give careful thought and consideration to the aspects of life that truly fill your soul. Intentionality of deliberate decision-making and redirection, commitment to a persistent positive approach, strong time management and goal prioritization are keys to any rebalance platform. Formulating new patterns involves looking at our pre-existing paradigms and routines. In order to execute positive change, we must be *deliberate decision makers* that *construct and not destruct our lives.* Commit to doing a self-evaluation and weekly audits to maximize your results.

Self-Evaluation Audit Questionnaire

The self-evaluation questionnaire provided below is designed to assist individuals in a personal rebalance strategy. Conduct a detailed inventory of your personal and professional life assets and liabilities. This is not a reflection of how you want your life to look like, but a realistic depiction of what in fact truly exists. Pivotal questions will assist you in arriving at a "realistic self-examination and evaluation."

Analyze your patterns and routines on what you do on a daily basis and established time allotments. Observe the impact of how you feel after each specific activity.

So you may ask why some individuals achieve so much, while others struggle to do the minimum. Top performers, adversity over-comers and successful individuals succeed through following clear strategic action plans and avoid wasting energy on lower return objectives or suffering from analysis paralysis. These individuals do not succumb to downward spirals or chaos, they vigorously manage their schedules and agendas to edit out distractions or derailment. *Results based thinking (RBT) is the secret ingredient.* RBT focuses on accomplishing a specific goal or task, gaining maximum value for your time and effort. On the other hand, many people are plagued by their misperception that they have effectively achieved their goals, when the reality is opposite. I refer to this as "ineffective churning" whereby you can be busy accomplishing nothing. Similar to a dog chasing his own tail, it is a continuous process that renders no results to show for your time allocation and attention. *"Ineffective Churning"* is a common symptom of unbalance in our society creating anxiety and mass frustration. *Churners* are inefficient and often their behavior is indicative of an underlying issue, whereby misdirecting or diverting attention to deflect from other life issues they are not ready to acknowledge. It is therefore of critical importance for us to manage our energy reserves, ensuring we are both mentally and physically equipped to deal with life's challenges and unpredictability.

When overburdened with your current schedule and your personal and professional life feels as though it is in chaos, we begin to ask ourselves what is the first step we should take? How do I function given my current set of circumstances? Can I do things differently or what resources are necessary to change and improve things? When the heaviness of life feels as though it is going to suffocate you and there is no end in sight, how do you survive, let alone thrive? The concept of work/life rebalance seems illusive and out of reach for most individuals. *Rebalance* can be achieved when you are armed with the right tools and techniques.

Rebalance Techniques

One technique that can be employed to rebalance your life is "visualization." Close your eyes and systematically walk through the ideal utopia of your perfect rebalanced life. This process involves visualizing finite details, whereby imagining your life from the inception of your day to strategically review your routine. Envision certain time intervals when you wake up in the morning, to what exercise you do, even mundane tasks like the time you brush your teeth or take a shower. Vision boards are useful tools to create and illustrate a rebalanced life that you desire. The following are additional recommended techniques designed to assist your personal rebalance strategy.

> "Decide today that for the rest of your life you are going to formulate healthy rebalanced habits and establish a rebalanced routine to contribute to your life strategy" - Darcee McJannet

Personal Development Investment Yields Returns for Corporations

Individual success translates into organizational success. Globalization has changed the dynamics in our society. Displacement has become the norm and is forcing migration of individuals based on job relocation. The modern and often transient professional world has disconnected individuals from easily accessing strong family and community support structures that were historical coping mechanisms to deal with change and stress. As a result, the individual often must deal with challenges on their own or look to new avenues for support, such as their workplace or coaches. This is where organizations that want to be exemplary have to step up with work/life rebalance. Employees spend more hours per day at work than at home, which is why companies that create a *pseudo family* environment will win out in this competitive global economy. Top employers value their employees and recognize that creating a balanced or rebalanced culture in the workplace positively impacts the business financially and the personal lives of their employees. CEOs, executives and managers must recognize that employees are the life-blood of their organization. Without solid employees and leadership, businesses cannot effectively run, expand, or manage, thus negatively impacting the bottom line and market share. Treating your "human capital" well and creating a respectful and flexible workforce is just good business. The bottom line is a direct reflection of the inner workings of an organization. Your internal clients will drive your success. Retaining employees and professional knowledge workers that have a higher complexity position and skill set will require a significant investment, but a fraction of the cost that would be required to deal with high employee turnover and new employee training.

The Center for American Progress cited 30 case studies in 11 research studies, found, "it costs about one-fifth of a worker's salary to replace that employee, which result in significant costs that can potentially be avoided by implementing workplace flexibility and earned sick days at little or no cost at all." [2] Progressive organizations recognize that investing in work/life balance initiatives for personal and professional development render a much higher return on investment, than paying the hard fixed costs of replacing an employee. Turnover expense ratios are now being taken more seriously from an operational and human resources standpoint, due to the ability to quantify information that used to be qualitative in nature, relating to human development. The cost of recruitment, retraining, reputational costs, low morale and dissatisfaction with existing employees, and potential future loss of other employees feeling the unstable environment. The concept of "corporate wellness" is a timeless principle. The climate of your corporation or business dictates the degree to which your organization will prosper and grow. The case for rebalance in one's personal and professional environments will forever remain an essential need. A reported one quarter of working adults dislike their jobs. This translates into

---

[2] Center for American Progress, Article dated November 16, 2012 - There are significant costs to replacing employees, written by Heather Boushey and Sarah Jane Glynn

rebalance and flexibility being a key determinant for employee retention.

One means of assisting employees to achieve a rebalance/balanced life is through implementing and investing in a corporate wellness program. According to an article in *Forbes*, there are significant tangible benefits of a corporate wellness program (CWP):

> CWP has the potential to reduce an employee's chance of incurring key health risks such as obesity, high cholesterol and blood pressure, as well as the potential to help them stop smoking or abusing alcohol. Employees are also more likely to stay with a company they perceive to be making an investment in their well-being, according GreenIndustryPros.com.
>
> With those risks mitigated, companies could <u>cut their health care costs</u> by about $650 (or 18% per average working-age adult) and up to 28% for older adults and retirees, according to a study in the *Journal of Occupational and Environmental Medicine*.
>
> According to *Corporate Wellness Magazine*, <u>each dollar invested in a wellness program can yield about $4 in increased productivity,</u> with less absenteeism and lower insurance costs.
>
> The article cited a study by Wellness Proposals that found at companies where wellness programs were implemented, <u>sick leave was down by 28%</u>, use of health care benefits was lowered by 26%, and

compensation claims made by employees were reduced by 30%.[3]

Corporate wellness and other programs such as preventative care, are examples where corporations have taken initiative to invest in human capital development to assist employees rebalancing their body, mind, and spirit, resulting in positive returns to the employee and the financial bottom line of the company.

Achieving Personal and Professional Fulfillment

First and foremost, individuals must identify their strengths and weaknesses. Live consciously and avoid being a zombie of indecision and apathy. Going through the motions of life without direction and purpose will result in a person becoming a *"Directionless bystander,"* with few expectations and fewer personal successes. Exist in the moment, persist through challenges, resist negative thoughts, and consistently strive to rebalance your life through holding yourself accountable to your rebalance strategy. If you invest and focus on achieving a rebalanced life that enriches your mind, body and soul, you will limit the opportunity of energy depleting activities that lead to *"unbalanced unhappiness."* Be true to yourself, remain positive, meet your challenges head on, and thrive in your new rebalanced reality.

"A rebalanced lifestyle is its own reward." - Darcee McJannet

---

[3] Forbes website, Is a corporate wellness or preventive care program right for your company?, written by C.Hall, 02/06/2013

To contact Darcee:

Founder, CEO, Stratego Consulting International Inc.

International Coach, Author, Speaker www.darceemcjannet.com

strategoconsulting@gmail.com

(403) 850-1970

www.twitter.com/strategytogo

www.facebook.com/strategoconsulting

www.linkedin.com/pub/darcee-mcjannet

*Stay tuned for my upcoming book on successful work/life rebalance.

Julie Jones Hamilton

The founder of *The Empowerment Foundation Group, LLC,* and *Julie Jones Hamilton International Consulting,* Julie is a highly trained consultant specializing in global transformation principles and personal development. She consults professionals, groups, entrepreneurs and churches to create results, realize dreams, accelerate success and build lasting relationships by applying a 'thinking technology' in building a blueprint for a business and a life they love living.

She is co-author of the *Women Living Consciously II* series, *The Change* series and *Keys to Conscious Business Growth,* as well as co-founder of *The Four Dames*, who offer self-development interactive workshops, courses, spa retreats and currently co-authors of the soon-to-be-published book, *The 12 Absolute Laws of Creating Wealth.*

For the previous 24 years Julie has served thousands of women reclaim inner-power from substance dependency as former president and board member of the renowned long-term treatment facility, *The Chrysalis House*, in Lexington KY.

Julie is the recipient of Dream Builder Achievement Award of Excellence and the MAMLS Award from Gay Hendricks, Bob Proctor, Peggy McColl and Mary Morrissey.

She lives in Lexington Kentucky with her passion - beloved husband Jimmy, two married daughters, a college son and six grandchildren.

The Power of Change

Be A Deliberate Co-Creator of Your Life's Experience.

By Julie Jones Hamilton

I used to think I was rich and invincible when I was a multi-millionaire. Then I discovered, when it was all gone, the very true meaning of wealth.

What I discovered along the way is - there are two absolutes in the universe. The first absolute is, *everything* changes, the weather, the time, the money in our bank account, relationships, our age, everything.

The second absolute is - you and I have one hundred percent dominion over the thoughts we *choose* to think. Not dominion over thinking because thinking is a constant stream of consciousness and life is consciousness. However, we do have dominion over which thoughts we *choose* to think.

Now, some of you may already know this, yet so few know the *power* of knowing this. You and I have so much power when we focus our thoughts, when we focus on what we would love to be, do, have and create in our life by *choosing* to pay attention to what we are paying attention to. This is the beginning of deliberately utilizing our power by noticing the thoughts we are thinking.

My story is of incredible highs and excessive lows, which proves to me we live in a polarized universe. Up, down, hot, cold, day, night, as far down as you go is how high up you can go and even higher up, further still.

THE ESSENCE OF LIFE ITSELF

Growing up, I used to think if I worked really hard, did what I was told, was obedient and accommodating, things would work out; but I don't believe that anymore.

I have found that to create a successful, rich and meaningful life I must pay attention to my thinking and harness the energy of the thoughts that serve me. I must listen to my heart, and build muscles in trust and believing in the power of this benevolent, creative Energy in the universe to design a life I would love living.

Albert Einstein says: "The most important decision we make is whether we believe we live in a friendly or hostile universe."

I have discovered there is a spiritual side of success in living a life by design. When this is observed and practiced, one becomes the architect of a successful and prosperous life, a deliberate co-creator of one's life experience. To me this is *real wealth*.

Most people live a life on default, unaware of the expansive, creative power within each of us. I once heard, "We can live to be 90 years old or we can live one year 90 times." The choice is ours.

To sustain any real lasting change, it's up to me to take personal responsibility. I must make heartfelt decisions that align with my core values. Aligning my thoughts with certain fundamental principles is indeed the essence of life itself. It's life seeking to emerge.

This Energy of life is everywhere, and will break through concrete seeking the light.

So my job is to decide and choose thoughts, which allows me to become the best version of myself in action. It's the greatest gift to give myself and those I love. However, it's also the hardest work in the world.

One of my favorite authors, Wallace Wattles, writes in his book *The Science of Getting Rich, The Proven Mental Program to a Life of Wealth,* "There is no labor from which most people shrink as they do from that of sustained and consecutive thought; it is the hardest work in the world."

However, when I do this, I tap into this deep reservoir of Creative Power and I am able to deliberately co-create my life's experiences.

Some call this creative power Source, Infinite Intelligence, God, Buddha or the Field of Potential. It matters not what name is given to the invisible Formless Substance.

What matters is knowing that we all have access to and are capable of consciously generating this incredible Energy, which lives and breathes and has its being in you and in me. This is the essence of life itself.

I must admit, had I known beforehand the peaks and valleys I would be facing, I may not have been so willing to move through being worth millions of dollars, owning several companies, flying on private jets, dining with movie stars, dignitaries and senators, being invited to presidential inaugurations and being the guest of rulers in other nations, to watch it quickly disappear like sand through an hourglass with my claw marks all over it.

What I went through I wouldn't wish on anyone, but where it took me I would wish on everyone. What I learned is what is taught on the hero's journey, *the power of change.*

TO THY OWN SELF BE TRUE

Early on after two children, a divorce and a hospital stay for substance dependency, I made the decision to meditate and develop a relationship with my Higher Power. The more I developed this personal relationship, the more I shared my true self with others.

I found that when I am venerable, genuine and authentic, no matter how difficult it may seem to be, the results are always healing. I discovered a compass to live by in the words of Shakespeare, "To Thy Own Self Be True."

Anytime I vary away from this compass, no exceptions, I learn new and powerful lessons; sometimes gently, sometimes not so gently.

In developing a relationship with this Higher Power as a sober, single mother, I attracted a fine, southern gentleman, Jimmy. After a whirlwind courtship, he moved my two little girls and me from the sunny beaches of Southern California to the bluegrass state of Lexington, Kentucky. We married, had a son and reared a family.

During our marriage, my prosperous, vibrant Prince Charming provided for us richly. Jimmy and I owned three homes and luxury vehicles. Our children went to the finest schools in town and we traveled extensively.

As a volunteer and former board president of a women's dependence facility, I was privileged to serve and support others. I also enjoyed being on the board of trustees of my son's school while participating in other fundraising endeavors and making new and meaningful friendships.

At first, the unraveling began slowly and without notice; I wasn't paying attention. Then things began to fall apart. It dawned on me I had simply transferred my dependency of success onto outside circumstances and material possessions. I was in a trance.

"I WAS WALKING ALONG AND ALL OF A SUDDEN…"

When our son was young, any time something of importance happened to him, he always began his stories with, "I was walking along and all of a sudden…"

So, there I was, *"walking along and all of a sudden…"* My husband informed me he entered into a lawsuit with a company that had infringed upon his security software patent.

He believed he was right and was determined to prove it. For a man who had never lost before and with no "reverse" in his experiences, he plowed straight ahead into a long, exhausting and debilitating litigation with one of the most powerful companies on the planet - Google.

Needless to say, our entire fortune was systematically disassembled, and also that of our investors, based on what he knew was right. Afterwards, he shared with me what an "old-timer" once told him, "Just because you're right, Hamilton, doesn't mean you're gonna win!" Then my beloved husband turned around, walked into the bedroom, climbed into bed and stayed there for three and half years.

Operating in fear and conditioned based thinking, I scrambled to do what I could with what I had. I began to sell what we owned of value - art, property, jewelry, etc. - in hopes my Jimmy would awake from his sleep in time to rescue me.

A part of me wanted to be the one in bed with covers over my head. My continued thoughts were, "How can I get money to pay for the house bills and food, I'm not educated with a career? How can I make money? How do I support our family, how, how, how?"

It's a funny thing when I place my dependency on outside circumstances and conditions; I tend to forget I am the cause of my effects. The illusions, which appear, seem so real at the time. They may even be facts, but the truth is, I have a Power greater than any illusions. Either the change will have me or I will have the change.

What I know now is, I have a choice. If I leave it up my own ego, I will choose victimhood and begin thinking, "Life is happening to me." Or I will place my dependency on my Higher Power, let go of the resistance and remember, "Life is happening through me, as me."

WAKING UP TO THE POWER OF CO-CREATING

Early one morning, walking into our darkened bedroom while my husband slept, I suddenly knelt down and prayed, asking my Higher Power for a deeper understanding and the strength to create a new life.

Moments later as I entered the bathroom, I heard a still small voice, which I hadn't heard for a while clearly say, "Relax, I go before you." The overwhelming sense of gratitude I felt in hearing this familiar voice was like the sweet breath of fresh air.

Caught up in the drama of my story I somehow lost my compass, which happens to many of us when we are not noticing what we are noticing.

Then and there I made a resolve to up level my thinking and bring gratitude, appreciation and love into every aspect of my life.

With my compass in hand, I saw clearly I had misplaced my dependency upon outside conditions and the material world. I ceased using my precious resources, my vivid imagination, visualization, intuition and faith. I saw my complacency in being stuck in lack and limitation.

I allowed the power of change to have me. In any given moment, at any given time, we have the power and the capacity to change, if we are willing. The choice is ours.

My one and only desire was to bridge the invisible side of my nature with the human side of my nature and create a new story of a life I love living.

THE GAP

We all must go through a place called "The Gap" when we deliberately co-create a new, more powerful life. The gap is what life looks like here, when what we would love is over there. In between is the gap; the space where change takes time.

Because everything is energy in the universe we live in, our thoughts hold powerful energy. This is science as described in quantum physics. Because thoughts are consciousness and the world we live in is made up of pure consciousness, our thoughts will become the forms we think about most.

Our conditions and circumstances begin to change in accordance to our observations. This is why it is of the utmost importance to notice what we're noticing, to notice the thoughts we are thinking because thoughts are things.

While in the gap, I continue to hold the focus on the images of my desires, on the story of the new life I would love, while in everyday living. Doing this, the molecules of my old life begin to dissolve from lack of attention and will then rearrange themselves into the patterns of the images I am focusing on. This takes willingness, commitment and a burning desire.

Ralph Waldo Emerson shares in his quote, "Stand guard at the portal of your thoughts." - And "Nothing is at last sacred but the integrity of your mind."

In my decision to change, I became earnest in my daily spiritual practice, I let go of my victim story and limiting beliefs to create a space to dream again. Relying upon the truth that life is not happening to me, life is happening *through* me, my life began to shift.

I then created a vision statement of a life filled with confidence, joy and freedom, vibrant health, financial abundance and a vocation I love. In doing so my life began to reflect the images in my vision.

A perfect example is while my husband lay sleeping and creditors were circling our wagon, I did what I could with what I had. I reached out to our creditors and made payment arrangements. I cleared out and cleaned out my home, selling and giving things away we no longer used or needed.

On my vision statement, which I read many times daily, I wrote down I would love five hundred thousand dollars and a black Lexus, along with other life giving experiences. I created a vision board with cut out words, pictures of this new life, money and a Lexus and put them on this board to support my daily focus.

Eighteen months later, though a series of events such as a sale of a property, payment from a remaining patent and a tax-free financial gift, five hundred and six thousand dollars was in our bank account. A few months after that, my stepfather bought a new car and gifted me his, which happened to be a beautiful black Lexus.

This is but a couple of the many occurrences that continue to happen in several various ways in my new life all because I choose to be a deliberate co-creator of my life's experience.

Now, I could not have *made* them happen; however, I did make them *welcome*.

THE SPIRAL OF MY BECOMING

In the spiral of my becoming, I realize I am the cause of the effects in all of my experiences. Through this understanding, I am given the opportunity to work with the Power in my life.

When I pay attention to what I am paying attention to and I focus my thinking on thoughts that give me life, I find new ideas and actions to create a joy-filled life. In practicing this principle in all my affairs, I create experiences of my heart's desires and so can you.

Working with the understanding of the Law, Energy, Source, Infinite Intelligence or God, whatever words used to identify the invisible Formless Substance in which we live in, anything is possible.

In the words of Napoleon Hill, "Whatever the mind can conceive and believe, it can achieve."

Einstein once said if he had to answer a question in one hour and his life depended on it, he would spend fifty-five minutes on the question and within five minutes he would have the answer.

There is nothing you can think of that the mind in which you thought it up with would know exactly how to bring it about. So my question would be… "What do I love?" What would I love to be, do, have and give in my life?

WHAT DO I LOVE?

My work today is to stay curious and think of the most powerful questions in any given situation, which is, "What do I love?"

While creating a new career with three companies, I made a conscious decision to hold my husband in truth and repeat out loud daily, "I behold you in the eyes of love and I glorify in your wholeness."

I truly believe in my husband's gifts and talents, his millionaire mindset, and in the Power that is breathing in him, and by God, we plan to love our way back into millions.

So it was of no surprise to me when, at the end of my husband's depression, he slipped into an accidental overdose with prescribed medications and was placed in ICU. On the second morning, I came to visit he grabbed my hand and whispered, "You won't believed what happened to me last night!" and proceeded to share with me an amazing story.

While he was sleeping, he saw himself wrestling and finally in the distance saw a *Light* and crawled in it. Then the most remarkable things occurred.

He said this *Light* was filled with love and euphoria and showed him all the good he had done in his lifetime that he had long ago forgotten. Between sobs and tears he tried to explain what he experienced in the presence of this *Light*. In 20 years of marriage, I had not seen this version of him before.

"It is beyond human language and I have no words to describe it," he said of this feeling of pure love. I could tell by his revelation he was not delusional and what I was witnessing was a healing of Biblical proportions.

After his release from the hospital I noticed the extreme difference in him. He began to attend daily mass at the church he grew up in. He began to exercise and swims every other day. After several years,

I watched my husband return to his vital, funny and happy self in which he remains today.

His experience proved to me *the power of change.*

To some, what may seem like a tragic story of a rich couple is, indeed, the story of a couple discovering true riches. Gifted with the opportunity of incredible highs and excessive lows, we discovered a much deeper connection within ourselves and with each other.

We all have the capacity to embrace and use the power of change with ease and grace or with resistance and claw marks. I know because I've done both.

It's in the allowing and letting go that real changes take place. Change is an absolute and we each have 100% absolute dominion over the way we choose to look at change. I choose to look at it as an opportunity today.

I live a very wealthy life in an abundant universe with the people I love. I am supported while in business and in life as I help support my family, friends and clients in the power of change by staying in the most important question of all and asking, "What do you love?"

To contact Julie:

859-229-5939

Julie@JulieJonesHamilton.com

www.JulieJonesHamilton.com

www.FourDames.com

Amberli Hartwell

Amberli set up and ran one of the first complimentary health centers in Scotland in her twenties. Her original interest in holistic health came from her search to be free from chronic fatigue syndrome. Having gone through her own journey of healing from childhood sexual abuse, she acts as a catalyst for people who have had a raw deal but don't want their history to define them.

She is experienced and qualified in massage, SHEN (emotional release therapy), holistic life coaching, feng shui and meditation.

Amberli looks for that pivotal point where instead of being pushed by your pain you start to be pulled by a vision, to give your life new direction. She has helped thousands of people overcome often extremely challenging situations, and supported her husband in closing his 150-year family business in order to follow his lifelong dream to live in New Zealand.

Amberli has been featured in magazines, radio and newspapers and before emigrating gave talks at Country Living magazine's spring fair. She was also chosen for the television show, "The Peacemakers," which took 2nd place in an international TV format competition.

Non-local clients to Nelson, New Zealand, stay and work with her daily; Amberli travels regularly or can hold consultations via Skype. She created "9 Steps To Cloud9" in recognition of the need for self-reference and direction in personal development.

9 Steps to Cloud 9

By Amberli Hartwell

I stood on our deck mesmerized by the sparkles of light dancing on the sea. The tide never rushes yet it's always on time; it patiently ebbs and flows in a rhythm that echoed our slow, long journey of bureaucratic challenges. The words of the deportation letter we had just received were ringing in my ears, "Please leave the country in five weeks." My husband Jim was sitting on the edge of our bed reading and re-reading the letter with disbelief, knowing all too well just how much we had given up to be here. We had reached the end of the road and my efforts to help Jim with his lifelong dream of moving to New Zealand had failed.

Feeling defeated, I started mentally planning the return to Scotland. How would I break the news to our young girls? By now they had settled in and were making friends, as were we. But my imagination couldn't conjure up what that would be like. As a last gasp, I remembered my waning belief that dreams do come true. To give myself focus, I asked, "What does New Zealand residence look like?" - and there it was - this IS New Zealand, and we are already residing in it! Clear as day, the "residence" we wanted was only a piece of paper, and one we had to get. Thanks to friends and people in positions of power who listened, we are now not only bona fide New Zealand residents, but New Zealand citizens.

When you are not in the situation you want to be in, it can be difficult to imagine that things could be any different, to the point where all you can see is what you don't want and that is usually precisely what you have.

No matter what your external circumstances may be now, I encourage you to build a working relationship with your inner and outer world, because life is less about what the eye sees and more about what the soul feels. Your thoughts, assumptions and feelings can then no longer shove you from pillar to post, but instead, the light of your awareness leads you on a journey to your dream that fulfills and empowers you to blossom into who you really are. The external reflection of your life then aligns with this new you, creating for yourself a fulfilling reality designed by your heart.

The default setting most people live life by is to find someone - anyone, anything, to blame for making them feel bad and for life not going their way. This distraction may bring temporary alleviation, but carries the burden of long-term stuck-ness; yet all is a ploy to avoid turning inwards. By instead learning to observe the changes in your external life as a mirror of your internal world, you have the perfect gauge for your awakening potential. Listening to your inner intuition as your personal guide, you can close your ears to naysayers and be a co-creative life designer instead. With your life as your personal friend and mentor, you discover that inherent within your chosen dreams realization, rests your sleeping potential.

A wise old man came to me one night in a dream and said, "Amberli, you already know how to make dreams come true, so it is time for you to learn the theory behind it." He went on, "The moment you give birth to a dream, you start a process of creation. You may believe your dream doesn't exist at this stage, but that's not true. Your dream has its own wavelength, like this," and he drew waves from a picture of a house high up across the page. "You also have your own wavelength," and he drew a person with different shaped waves lower down the page. "For any dream to come true, all you have to do is lift your wavelength up to your dreams same frequency and then it will manifest in the material world. If your dream has not come true, then that means you are not yet a match to its higher wave-length, that is all." I woke up and knew I had just been given the missing key that made sense of my entire life.

This vital language of energy is often overlooked. It is replaced by lots of opinions from the masses, if you listen to all that advice you could end up chasing your tail. Rather than becoming an expert at dealing with setbacks with boxing gloves on, you will feel motivated and more connected to yourself if you are tuned into your dream and are willing to trust that your life, i.e. your mentor, has chosen the perfect route for you.

Your wavelength is where your true power for personal growth and change lies and is heightened or lowered by:

Your feelings:

Some emotions sink you: e.g., fear, low self-esteem, and some uplift: e.g., joy, confidence.

Your thoughts and words:

Words are like seeds and can either grow flowers or weeds: "flowers" will uplift, and "weeds" will sink, but both grow.

Your perspective:

You may not be able to change your situation immediately, but you can always change the angle you are looking at it; and that can help you see what to do.

Your desires:

Validate and own your desire.

Your focus:

Whatever you focus on increases.

Your beliefs:

When all beliefs are gone, all that is left are infinite possibilities!

Like attracts like. Raising your wavelength is the quickest way to attract change, opportunities, people who can help you, and favorable circumstances.

So join me on a symbolic journey in a hot air balloon! Why? To represent the raising of your wavelength, and also because a hot air balloon rises not through force, but through allowance. Like a rhythmic dance, rather than a set protocol to follow, the process requires you to adapt your response moment to moment according to each stage.

Let's face it, a hot air balloon is probably the most impractical mode of transport available - you wouldn't exactly use it to go shopping! Its sole reason for existence is to give the people it carries an incredible experience. This is the same as your life - you are here for the journey, rather than to reach a specific destination. As soon as you truly accept your life as a journey, the pressure to produce results releases, so you can make friends with every stage. Ironically, this makes reaching cloud9 easier!

Just as your wavelength and all the inner aspects you align to create a fulfilling life are invisible, so is the air inside your hot air balloon. The balloon rises because warm air is lighter than cold air. Just as air is everywhere, supportive, life-giving even, yet taken for granted, so too is this inner "air." It contains everything you need, but you have likely been conditioned to believe only in what you can see and not what you can feel. Therefore, "action leads to results" is all you have to go by and aspire to, but finished products are tangible symptoms that mirror realized potential. If you don't have them and want them, then there is more of you to discover!

If you can relate to being down on the ground with your basket upturned and your balloon deflated and maybe even burst, you are probably wishing your dream would come down and rescue you. Although on the one hand that might be great, on the other, you would miss out on the most exquisite personalized development program designed for you to expand into the fullness of who you really are.

You may now be asking, so how can I get myself from here to up there?

Step 1 - Defy The Forces Of Gravity:

Your wavelength naturally wants to raise, it is not something you need to force, but rather allow to happen by getting out of your own way. You can do this by dropping whatever weighs you down and aspiring to what lifts you up. If you want to live a renewed life, you may need to let go of, for example: trying to please everyone else by realizing you are not pleasing anyone, not even yourself. This is the threshold of self-responsibility that every dreamer must cross.

The good news is that when you let go of what you *don't* want and start to focus on what you do want, opportunities rush in to meet and greet you.

Step 2 - Name and Claim Your Cloud9

There is no doubt that if you know what you want, the delivery is much faster; but not everyone knows what they want. The more disillusioned you are by life, the less you can see beyond what you have. Nonetheless, life has no opinion whether your dreams are too large or small. Your desires still accumulate on cloud9 in etheric form waiting for you to align with them, so they can manifest. All that you want has been channeled into here, not only through you deliberately asking, but also through the unconscious desire within you for life to be different. Every difficulty you have had, has in some way contributed to your cloud9 forming. Those painful life experiences caused you to desire the opposite. So when you experience hardship, abundance waits for you to discover it on cloud9; if you are physically suffering, then health and wellness is there for you; and so on. You can still raise your wavelength without knowing what your cloud9 looks like. As you let go, you start to see more clearly.

Step 3 - Heat Your Balloon

Any dissatisfaction you feel about your current life is a healthy sign that you can hear your heart crying and are ready for change. To inspire means "to breathe life into," so do whatever it takes to heat your heart with your passion for cloud9. As your internal fire flares, your heart stirs just like the metaphorical balloon as it awakens and changes shape from dull, flat and lifeless to buoyant, vibrant and exciting. Give your heart a voice; feel the intense pull from your soul and let love take over. What fascinates and thrills you? Find the core flame that burns in your heart. When are you most alive? Connect with what uplifts you and put your focus there. Park your practical worries and visualize the life you want with fervor. Feel every cell inside you dance with joy and excitement and wake your heart up. Channel that into your visualized dream so you can feel your heart expand like the balloon.

Just as your balloon carries the basket and not the other way round, your mind becomes the servant of your heart and surrenders to the malleable fascinating route your heart is taking you. If you are used to sticking to plans, this may feel strange. However, when you make a plan without being flexible, you limit possibilities from elsewhere that don't fit your plan, but could be even better. When you don't resist and instead switch to trusting and allowing your heart to guide you through life, everything flows. With your heart stirring as your wavelength lifts, thoughts of hope and fresh ideas emerge.

Step 4 - Get In The Basket

The basket is pulled upright by the warmth of your heart, so climb in and commit to your dream happening. Like the warm air focused into the balloon above you, you hold and contain your vision in your heart.

To allow for a flexible take off, many wicker strands are woven together forming this lightweight basket. You cannot rely on a basket with holes in it to carry you to cloud9! Therefore, your individual thoughts need to be supportive and work harmoniously to be flexible and gentle towards yourself, so your heart can carry you up to cloud9. This lighter way of being is very different to disciplining yourself to try harder. Being aware of your thoughts and words is important to prevent sabotaging yourself and your dreams. Anyone who helps you should also encourage you and not be destructive.

Step 5 - Identify Your GAS

Every journey requires fuel, even one in a hot air balloon! Your **G**ifts, **A**bilities and **S**kills awaken with your passion for cloud9.

Your unique **Gifts** are inherent within - you may have been born with them or gained them through life experience.

Your **Abilities** will blend your gift and skills creatively, and are developed by your desire for your dream.

Your **Skills** can either be deliberately learned, or acquired through experience. This is the only part of your development schools focus on! It is one-third of only one aspect, so if you feel like you are a failure, then maybe school has failed you. You may identify skills that might help make your dream come true or be useful for when it comes true, so either learn from a teacher you like or delegate that part to someone who has that skill.

Step 6 - Release the Ropes

Another reason people don't even reach for their dream is because of their limiting, self-imposed beliefs. These often form early on in life in response to dealing with a difficult situation, sometimes something way beyond your childhood comprehension. In a futile attempt to protect yourself from going through a painful experience again, you may have decided something is and always will be a certain way. It's likely you don't remember what you thought or perhaps even what happened, because this belief sinks into your unconscious mind and dictates your life without you knowing it. You are then locked into a world where other possibilities can't enter. This further confirms your belief and then your subsequent thoughts weave round that, keeping your wavelength low and setting up your reality as you don't want it. Just like the ropes that at first stabilize the basket and balloon before full take off... but if not released - prevent lift off, so too, do those beliefs... until you become aware of and release them. With the ropes still in place, you can't express your passion and you will experience frustration, and eventually your passion frizzles out too. Living life free from those limitations is like releasing the ropes so you can lift off!

Step 7 - Pull the Cord

Skills and taking action are normally the only two areas you are told about when trying to make a dream come true. Do you think you need more confidence before you can take action? That will keep you stuck, because nothing actually happens without you taking any action, and when nothing happens your confidence sinks. To break this cycle, take action to allow the gas through to fuel your passion and watch your confidence soar and your skills develop as you go.

When your inner world is being taken care of and you are open to your outer world's response, you will be amazed at how much easier your life flows. The action you take is therefore, aligned with what you are passionate about, so it is enjoyable and not a chore (so you don't gas yourself to sleep)! This makes what you do far more effective and productive, yielding results more quickly and beyond your wildest imaginings.

Step 8 - Go With the Flow

A hot air balloon doesn't necessarily take a direct route to anywhere, it generally moves up and along, but sometimes to gain height may need to drop to align with the wind to push it in a favorable direction. These moments of dropping are like the times when your progress seems to be going backwards, but you don't realize this is, so you will be swept along.

Sometimes your flexibility around your plans is challenged as you are invited to surrender to a path you can't see. This can be when there is a divine plan that sits outside of the one you cooked up, which will challenge you to let go of yours. When nothing works out no matter how hard you try, this is often the reason. Trusting the flow, intuitively responding to the shifts and discovering the freedom and joy this wind can offer you, is a vital part of reaching your dream. Often, we think we are making a dream come true by having an A B C plan for how the dream is going to happen - and in what order - but if you can learn to be carried by this wind, your journey will be far more exciting as you arrive at cloud9.

Step 9 - Reach Cloud9

There can be a wobbly time when cloud9 nears and fantasy is about to become reality, but you can't yet see the details. This stage is like when the balloon goes through cloud9, but you haven't arrived on cloud9 yet, and giving up may be tempting. To give yourself the final push, celebrate and be grateful for every little thing in your life, because attitude and aptitude = altitude! Sit tight and enjoy the ride and ensure you are kind to yourself, because this is when your fear of success may want to sabotage what is about to come.

When your basket reaches cloud9, you will look back and see the magic of the journey; but soon you will look up and move toward cloud 18, 28, 36… using and expanding on the skills you gained on the way to cloud9! By the time you reach cloud108, you will have found joy in helping other people. Any "toys" you gained may have lost some of their novelty value as you start to see that people and relationships are what matters far more than things. This is where the spiritual aspect of life has to enter for you to feel your life has meaning; otherwise, all will seem pointless. Helping another will bring new life to yours.

So the aim is to reach cloud9, and knowing when to put what effort where, is the art of the journey… as well as the art of discovering the real you.

To contact Amberli:

www.amberlihartwell.com

email:ask@amberlihartwell.com

www.facebook.com/AmberliHartwell

www.linkedin.com/in/amberlihartwell

www.twitter.com/AmberliHartwell

+64 (0) 3 5266 108

021 627 070

Insights Into Self-Empowerment

Sadie Allie

Me, in a nutshell: nutshell is too small. I have 51 years of experiences living this charmed life. That is what several of my acquaintances called my life: charmed. I tend to look at it a little differently. I have noticed that some people pre-judge too quickly and make assumptions.

My life has been filled with over 2 dozen places I've called home. I feel blessed I could love and raise 5 amazing children to adulthood. My soul connection with partners in my life has taken me to emotional places I cherish, and some places I desire never to revisit.

The essence of me is love, extreme happiness, silliness, compassion, adventurist, respect and seeker of understanding. My core values and desire to share my journey has led me here, and I am ready to give my greatest gifts. Opening up to share the things I know and understand is a risk I am willing to take. There are great messages and truth to confess and open the doors to new perspectives.

I currently find my joy in the early morning sun with a simple cup of coffee in hand, cuddling with someone I love, and forever laughing.

Behind Closed Doors

By Sadie Allie

I lay paralyzed with an ache I cannot even describe. My body felt limp, and my mind was consumed with a sensation of numbness. I was supposed to be watching the hockey game, something I never missed. As I lay there silently, I questioned how I could be feeling like this. It came out of nowhere! I was overwhelmingly immobilized. The dull pain raged through my body and pinned me to the bed.

The next morning I felt normal again. Without a second thought, I began my day with a great sense of energy and joy. I received a message from a friend who asked me to call Joe, a family friend who was an officer at the local sheriff's office in the town where my ex-husband Steven and my 12 year old son Jake lived. This sleepy little farming town had been my home for years. I called with an apprehension and concern for both of them. The next few minutes and years to follow, have changed everything about me, my life, and my family's lives.

Joe answered the phone and immediately got to business. "Steven has been murdered."

My knees buckled and I dropped to the floor. Before I could get any words out, his next comment took my breath away. "We have Jake in custody and are holding him as a suspect."

The tears and the unrecognizable moans of anguish escaped my body with no ability to stop them. I shook uncontrollably and fought back the urge to throw up.

I asked him in disbelief, "What? What do you mean? How? I don't understand!"

Joe explained as much as he could without divulging too much. My questions were many and the answers given to me incomplete and vague. He described the phone call my son made, the events that followed, and the condition of my son. Fear was spreading through the community of a killer on the loose. My son, numb and in shock, had told the story of an intruder. Before the sheriff arrived, my son had cleaned up as much as he could, changed his clothes, and then waited outside for the sheriff to arrive. The shooting had taken place the night before, at the exact time I lay unable to move.

The truth was that my son had shot and killed his father! They kept Jake up all night and through noon the next day, with no sleep, questioning him, not letting up until he admitted he did it. No one was there to represent him or support him. After the sheriff's office got what they needed from him, my son was turned over to the Juvenile Department of Corrections. Joe gave me the numbers to all the departments to contact Jake, the assigned attorney, and his personal number if I had other questions. In the moment I hung up the phone, my mind raced with disbelief, anguish, panic, and the maternal instinct to get to my son as soon as possible.

I was not in the states when this took place, and I needed to get back quickly. The relationship I was currently in was all that held me together at that moment. I was in a state of shock, incomprehensible pain, and disbelief. As I fell apart, Julian held me and consoled my soul, my heart, and advised me on the next steps to be taken. He arranged my flight back home and prayed to God above with me. That evening when I was allowed to talk with my son, I made the call. I eased my disposition with a very stiff drink and prepared for the unexpected.

I had not had a decent conversation with my son for over 18 months. The last words he spoke to me were several months previous with a frustrated and irritated tone. The words he spoke to me months ago still cut deep to my heart.

"I don't want you to call me anymore. Leave me alone. I don't ever want to see you again."

This conversation was one of only four conversations I was allowed to have with Jake during the last 18 months. As with every call before, I would cry to God above, to Julian, to my other adult children, friends, and even my ex-husband, begging and pleading to see my son. I did not understand why or how he could possibly not want to see me. We had been so close. We did everything together: Scouts, visits with friends, and movies with his siblings. There were always trips to town, school events, sports, yard work, errands for his dad and our business, projects, and more. He was my Jake and I loved him beyond measure. We would laugh, make videos, create art projects, piano lessons, and play the Wii.

After the drink took effect, I finally made the call to my son, my heart pounding in my chest, I waited for the voice on the other end of the line. I was told not to talk about what happened, just to let Jake know I was there for him. When Jake came on the line, he said two things that spun me into a twilight zone of bewilderment.

"Mom, I love you. I got your letters."

He had not said he loved me for 18 months, and I could not understand what letters he was referring to, since I sent so many. We only talked a few minutes, his voice calm and clear. He repeated those two statements several times adding to the questions in my mind. He said he was okay and asked when I would be there. I let him know I was heading back and would call him again the next day. As we ended our conversation, I spoke again with the staff at the center and asked about his disposition. The man on the phone said he was calm and emotionless. As a precaution, they put him on suicide watch. I hung up the phone and was incredibly sick. What the hell happened to my son?

After my flight back into the states, I made my way to see Jake. Again, advised by his court assigned lawyer not to talk about what happened. I took my oldest daughter with me. She also had experienced grief, anxiety and panic the few days before the shooting and felt relief after it happened with no idea why. The connection she and I felt to Jake was undeniable. We hugged my son as we entered, and sat in chairs facing Jake. We talked nonsense for a few minutes and then Jake's face flushed; he pulled at his eyelashes, as he always did when he had hurt feelings or anxiety. He turned to look at the bailiff and returned his gaze to me.

As his eyes welled up with tears, I calmly said to him, "I know we can't talk about it, but we will soon."

I hurt so much in that moment for my son. I wanted to give him that release, to allow him to pour out his heart to me and tell me what happened, not just that night, but over the last 18 months. We were not allowed that freedom.

I disagree with the judicial system in this case 100 percent. The system should have allowed me and my son a moment alone to reconnect and bond again to give him the opportunity to say anything he wished about what happened. He needed the safety of his mother's presence. I have always had an open and honest relationship with my son, encouraging him to talk to me about anything. The openness was taken away, first by his father and then by the courts. My son was not treated for shock and was left alone with his truth. Comments were made about his disposition. They would say to me, he is numb and emotionless. He is not reacting to the horrifying act he committed. He reacted to his pain, his suffering, and injustice of his father. I saw his emotion as we sat together the first time in 18 months. I felt his pain and felt as trapped as he did in pushing the emotions deep and carrying on idle conversations about nothing.

The next 6 months were spent in and out of the courtroom. The ending verdict listed as an undetermined amount of time spent in the Juvenile Department of Corrections. When the verdict came, Jake and I were allowed, for the very first time, to share an hour together without being supervised in the facility where he was being held. I was able to ask the hard questions, to discuss his reasons for his choice in actions. Too much time had passed. His being forced to not open up to me for the last 6 months made it difficult. I walked away that day not understanding everything and questioning even more.

Through counseling and many very brief conversations, I have learned some of the events that led to Jake's incomprehensible actions. The letters he referred to were letters he discovered as he was rummaging through a pile of newspapers for a school art project, three days before the shooting. My letters to him telling him how much I loved him, missed him, and of good times together. He ended up searching the house and found other letters, which only added to his anger and confusion about the lies his father had told him. These were Jake's words, not my assumption.

A child is not a pawn to be forced into removing a loving parent from his/her life. Threats, abuse, lies and deceit by my son's father drove him to take things into his own hands and trade his childhood for the right to love his mother and siblings again. Again, this is not my interpretation, but words from my son. He wanted all of us back in his life and made a very emotionally based choice. This was an act of survival and passion. His father loved him very much, but he never liked or understood Jake's relationship with me or his siblings. My ex-husband admitted to me he was jealous of the relationship I had with my four children from a previous marriage. He was also jealous of the love and admiration Jake had for his brothers and sisters. When my kids would visit, my ex would disappear into the family room and remove himself from all of us. It hurt Jake deeply when we were divorced, and it was hard on him to go from my home back to his dad's. He would tell me he did not want to leave to return to his dad's. I would encourage him to love his dad and to help him. He had us both forever. I hurt for Jake, but believed his father would do all he could to help him as I was doing.

Like any divorce, it is important to help your child work through the hard days, the confusion, and the heartache he or she feels when leaving one parent's home to go visit the other. My ex-husband chose to end my contact with my son only six months after the divorce, and he openly displayed his own negative feelings about me and the divorce in front of my son. The truth was never talked about with Jake. To my knowledge, the truth about why Steven and I had divorced was most likely never shared with anyone my ex-husband had in his life. Steven loved "fish" tales and I listened to him for 13 years twist the truth to suit his own needs. I listened to him lie to his family, his friends, people he worked with and more. These stories and lies about me would only add to the confusion and the pain for Jake.

After my ex was shot, the rumors were ridiculous. The comments of others hurt my kids; I told them to stop reading them. Ignorance was rampant. People always assume they know what happens behind closed doors, but I lived with this man for 13 years and there are many things only I knew, and many things only my son experienced. No one, including his grandparents, ever supported or stood up for Jake's right to be with me, his mother. No one ever contacted me about Jake with concern for his well-being. In my eyes, this was an act of neglect and cruelty to a child. I understand that when a person only has half the story from one parent, it can be difficult to reach out and get the rest of the story from the other parent. But, I am here to validate that it is vital. I take full responsibility for allowing Steven to play his best poker game ever and bluff his way to keep Jake and me apart. But, in the end, everyone lost that game.

My mistakes are hindsight. I, as a parent, had all the rights to be in my son's life. But, I was so trusting and believed every word my ex would tell me. You would think, of all people, I would know better. I was encouraged by my children to just go get Jake. I can honestly say that given the chance to go back, I would not have hesitated to go see my son and spend the time with him I was entitled to, even if it meant bringing along law enforcement. I did not intentionally abandon my son; I missed him every day of my life and still do today.

I was told time and time again by his father, "Leave him alone. He is happy. You would not even recognize him. He's not the same kid. If you come here you won't find him because he does not want you in his life."

Instead of calling bullshit and forcing my stand, I curled up in a fetal position and cried with such pain and heartache time and time again. This was my son! I knew he loved me. I was devastated and allowed my relationship with Jake to be manipulated.

It has taken me three years to find my stand, my voice, my truth. Although this is far from over for my son and me, the very core of my soul knows I must share my truth and empower others.

Ironically, in 2009, I worked with a life coach developing a series of DVD's to distribute to home day cares, schools, and church groups for caregivers and children. The idea behind the program was to teach caregivers and children the ability to recognize a call for help, to use their voices and to share their truths. A child will suffer in silence, but a child will speak volumes if someone is tuned in to the unspoken words.

Some of us have an ability to feel that something is amiss. We may not always know what it is, but those of us who are compassionate and have the ability to become present in the moments we are with others, can sense the energy being put forth. There are circumstances where the one closest to the abuser does not see it as it truly is. Sometimes the voice of the one being abused is lost in the conformity just to survive another day. I myself have lived a childhood of abuse and neglect and learned to suffer in silence.

Today, I have opened myself up to share this story only to help others take a truthful look at their relationship with their ex-spouse and their children. The importance of a strong sense of being loved by both parents and a respect of each child's rights is needed more than ever. We cannot afford as a society to continue to stand by and witness the deterioration of the family, especially when we are talking about families of broken homes.

Each parent, as an individual, has the responsibility and right to love, teach, and be part of their child's life. We do not have to agree on minor details, but we do have to agree to support our children to learn right from wrong, good choices and bad, and to gain the ability to be compassionate and love each other. If we help our children work through their feelings and learn how to communicate by speaking their truth with compassion, we will help mold an honest and compassionate adult. Making a decision to remove one parent because a child is dealing with confusing or angry feelings about the situation at that moment in time, is not a healthy or empowering choice.

As I move forward with my son and we find a renewed bond, I have encouraged him to find his voice of truth. My truth is not only my faults and mistakes, but the understanding of what was missing from my relationship with my ex-husband. Although, we are unable to force the communication and respect from our ex-spouse, we certainly have many resources and tools available to support our children through the reality of divorce. With so many divorced parents, single parents, and dysfunctional homes, the need has never been so great for a shift in how we communicate and are raise our children.

I will continue to write and speak, empowering and encouraging parents to strengthen the bonds to their children. Today is encompassed by plans of opening creative healing centers. I cannot emphasize enough the need to heal our hearts, speak our truths with compassion, and set aside trivial differences for our children. A child should ever have to experience separation from a loving parent, enduring abuse or neglect. A child should never have to experience the turmoil of his soul that lays claim on his childhood. Jake chose to end his silent suffering with his father, a choice he has ultimately regretted.

> *"A child was loved beyond measure. He only wanted the freedom to love also."* – Sadie

---

To contact Sadie:

www.sadieallie.com

www.facebook.com/SadieAllie

sadieallie@gmail.com

Carolyn P. Anderson

Carolyn Anderson is a co-founder and the Director of Global Family, a non-profit organization created in 1986, to shift consciousness to unity and love. Educator, author, speaker, and social pioneer, Carolyn is committed to the awakening of humanity to its full potential. Her passion is living and sharing the principles of co-creation and exploring the frontiers of evolutionary spirituality.

In her work with Global Family, she has coordinated activities for numerous global events, assisted with the creation of social cooperation trainings, and facilitated a number of international conferences and gatherings. By seeding the formation of hundreds of small Core Groups on five continents, she has empowered individuals all over the world to discover and fulfill their life purpose in support of the birth of a co-creative society.

In 1996, she co-founded Hummingbird Community in northern New Mexico to foster personal and planetary transformation. The Community is dedicated to modeling a co-creative culture in service to the evolution of consciousness.

Carolyn is a co-author of *The Co-Creator's Handbook*, the editor and co-creator of the *52 Codes for Conscious Self Evolution* with Barbara Marx Hubbard, and a co-founder of Living Co-Creation Associates, a social venture that empowers groups to embody the principles and practices of co-creation for their mutual awakening.

The Change That Changes Everything

By Carolyn P. Anderson

In the history of humanity, there have been only a small number of major transformations in human consciousness. These include the rise of foraging, hunting, and gathering 50,000 years ago; the advent of farming 10,000 years ago; the Age of Reason which birthed an era of rational thinking and scientific materialism in the 17th century and triggered the Industrial Revolution the last great shift.

From early Greek society through the time of scientist Sir Isaac Newton and the birth of classical physics 300 years ago even until today, the vast majority of humans have seen themselves as a body/mind, a mass of solid matter, a separate individual. As separate entities, humans feel that they must compete in order to win, or even survive, in an often unfriendly world of limited possibilities. Self-centered consciousness has been the norm.

This classical world view prevails even today for most of humanity. Organizations and institutions are based on hierarchy and a strict ordering of roles and responsibilities, all based on self-interest. Power manifests as domination over others, often through manipulation and control. Operating in these systems, individuals are largely disempowered and their creativity is stifled.

In addition to stimulating competition, the sense of being a separate self-fosters a belief in scarcity and the practices of hoarding, exploiting nature, and valuing money and possessions above life itself. It lies at the heart of human suffering, environmental destruction, and most of the problems faced by humanity. Whether it is the crisis in education, government, health care, or economics, the root cause is the belief that humans are separate from each other and from the natural world. This illusion of separation and its companion, self-centered consciousness, have proven to be disastrous! If left unchecked, this could lead to the sixth mass extinction to occur on this planet over its 5 billion year existence!

It is not difficult to see that humanity is at a crossroads! We must evolve or face the prospect of perishing as a species. The crises we face are serving as evolutionary drivers, challenging us to be more and to wake up to our true identity. As Einstein suggested, we cannot solve our problems using the same kind of thinking that created them. As the only species on Earth that can destroy all life as we know it, humanity has arrived at a turning point. We must shift from a consciousness of separation and fear to a consciousness of unity and love. We must move from relationships based on domination to relationships based on equality, mutual respect, empathy and non-violence. We must shift to a higher level of thinking, and we must move quickly. Humanity needs to take a quantum leap in consciousness.

Fortunately for our species and for our planetary home, a major awakening is occurring at this time. This current expansion of awareness was sparked a few decades ago by discoveries in the field of physics and the emergence of a new world view called conscious evolution.

Quantum physics has shown that humanity resides in a universe of infinite possibilities in which the observer creates reality. "What you see is what you expect." Intent thought itself determines outcome.

Humans are not separate powerless "cogs in a machine," rather we are multi-dimensional beings, unique aspects of the Force of Creation itself. We can affect something from a distance by the use of thought alone through the quantum field. We are more than our limited beliefs, emotions and physical bodies, we are directors of our own destiny and the destiny of the planet. We can transcend the sense of being a separate self to experience ourselves as unique aspects of the one Divine Intelligence.

When British biologist Rupert Sheldrake proposed his theory of morphic resonance, he suggested that a basic property of nature is that forms and patterns are contagious: once something happens somewhere, it can happen elsewhere because the invisible unified field connects everything. When individuals and small groups of people awaken in China, that occurrence affects citizens of the planet in every nation. We live in a relational universe. There are no boundaries when it comes to consciousness!

Emergence of The Co-Creator, The New Human

As circumstances on Earth dictate that we must either evolve or face possible extinction, a new kind of human is awakening and emerging "just in time." The predictions of great evolutionary spiritual pioneers such as Teilhard de Chardin, Sri Aurobindo, Barbara Marx Hubbard and others, are happening in our lifetime. A new kind of human is emerging. We call this person a Co-Creator,[4] a whole being who feels connected through the heart to all life and is awakening to the impulse to express unique creativity in service to the greater good. No longer operating from a sense of separation, the Co-Creator inhabits all the noble capacities of our species and is

---

[4] — Capital letters are used to describe this new person, to distinguish between the commonly used meaning of the words co-creator and co-creation. For most people, a co-creator is someone who cooperates with others and co-creation implies collaboration. Capitalizing Co-Creation as used here means conscious alignment with the impulse of creation—going beyond cooperation to mean Greater Self connecting to another Greater Self and to the natural world.

a new norm. The Co-Creator relinquishes the need for power over others and celebrates joining in authentic partnership with others in a spirit of unity, love and mutual respect.

The new human is part of a new story of creation a story of hope and infinite possibilities, a sacred narrative of an evolving universe of greater freedom and breathtaking creativity. Consciousness Divine Intelligence is always evolving and as consciousness incarnate, we are causal in the unfoldment of our lives and the fate of this planet. Through the power of our awareness, by focusing our attention and intention on what we choose and then allowing what follows to happen, we are creating a new reality.

The world view of conscious evolution shows us that we can evolve by choice, not simply by chance. Over the past billions of years and even during our lifetimes we have seen that crises always precede transformation. This is how evolution works: everything goes along as it is until difficult and disruptive circumstances create the necessity for a jump to the radically new, and a true transformation occurs. The problems that we face today are evolutionary drivers that can lead to innovation and genuine breakthroughs. The lessons of evolution have shown us that as living systems become more complex, they advance in consciousness, diversity, love, and freedom. In our increasingly complex world, we are evolving toward higher consciousness and greater love and freedom!

The Change That Changes Everything

This evolution of human consciousness and the shift from separation and fear to unity and love is the change that changes everything!

The new physics has taught us that everything is connected to everything else. We understand that our thoughts and actions have a powerful impact on all life, whether we are aware of this or not. As self-organizing inter-connected beings, we know that authority lies within and that our actions must flow from our inner knowing. This new understanding offers each of us the opportunity to find meaning and purpose in our lives and our time in history.

As we make this quantum leap in consciousness personally, our attention naturally turns to the good of the whole. We move from self-centered to whole-centered consciousness. We stop thinking, "either/or" to consider "both/and." Our identity shifts. We wake up. We become aware of ourselves as multi-dimensional beings unique and yet universal Co-Creators with the evolutionary impulse that created all that is, committed to birthing a healthy, thriving world based on caring, kindness and compassion for all.

From I To We: Empowering Our Mutual Awakening

Anthropologist Margaret Mead guided us with a formula for effective social change when she stated, "Never doubt that a small group of thoughtful, committed people can change the world; indeed, it's the only thing that ever has." To move beyond "change" to genuinely transform society, these "thoughtful, committed people" must take risks, go beyond linear process, and ignore the rules of the game. The civil rights movement, the women's movement, and the collapse of the Soviet Union are examples of social tsunamis where institutions that seemed intractable changed beyond imagination. They occurred because people thought and acted differently. They were ideas whose time had come!

How, we might ask, can we foster this kind of transformation to occur globally and in every sector of society? Individuals have been gathering in small groups for eons. It is neither predictable nor guaranteed that small clusters of people will be either effective or innovative. How can we take the chance out of this? Is there a process or model that we can follow to transform ourselves and society before we destroy civilization? Fortunately, I believe that the answer is yes. This may not be the only solution, but it is one solution that offers great promise as humanity stands on the brink of extinction.

In 1984, I was working with visionary Barbara Marx Hubbard[5] as a member of the management team that was guiding her "Campaign for a Positive Future." As we traveled around the US together, Barbara shared her vision with dozens of communities and small groups who had gathered to support her campaign. It was at this time that we "rediscovered" a divinely inspired pattern that we call the Core Group Process.[6] This model of Co-Creative principles and practices has provided a path for mutual awakening for indigenous people for generations and, in the past few decades, for thousands of small groups around the world. It offers a template for transformation based on the patterns of nature. It can be learned and replicated everywhere.

The groups that engage in this process are distinctly different from most others. Unlike groups that focus on personal growth and spiritual deepening but don't take action in the world, and unlike social action groups that don't take time to cultivate harmony and resonance among themselves, those who engage in this model bring together love and action - resonance and creative expression.

The process begins when individuals who are consciously evolving and are intent on expressing their full potential, join with one another. There is a recognition that although each of us is on a personal spiritual quest, all of us yearn for greater fulfillment and the experience of true family or community. In this step of the process, individuals focus on moving in consciousness from their egoic/personality selves to their essential divine nature. They begin

---

[5] Barbara Marx Hubbard is a speaker, author and social pioneer in the field of conscious evolution. She is co-founder of the Foundation for Conscious Evolution.
[6] The Core Group Process is described in detail in *The Co-Creator's Handbook*, co-authored by Carolyn Anderson with Katharine Roske and published by Global Family. The *Handbook* is available at www.thecocreatorshandbook.com.

to shift their identity in order to experience themselves as love incarnate, embodiments of the impulse of creation itself. This aspect of the process may take years, but it can be accelerated by putting focused attention on one's personal evolution and by being with "two or more" in a field of unconditional love.

It is love, the unifying and creative force of the Universe - the field that pervades all of Creation - that is the most essential component of the Core Group Process. Practices that support individuals to connect heart to heart and learn how to maintain and sustain resonance with others allow individuals within the group to move from a sense of separation to an experience of oneness.

Co-Creation is the process of accessing divine intelligence within Self and others; and it only occurs among co-equals in a field of trust, non-judgment and safety. It does not occur in a system of domination. The depth and beauty of each person is acknowledged through a practice of deep seeing, which empowers and calls forth the best in each member of the group. Through resonance, the group creates a coherent field, a "we space," which brings each member into the state of higher mind that Einstein suggested was essential for solving the problems we face collectively. Ordinary consciousness becomes expanded consciousness. This is why the Buddhist priest Thich Naht Hanh said that "The next Buddha may not be an individual, but an enlightened community." [7]

Because of the prevailing belief in the separate self and the fear that this engenders, it is essential for individuals and teams to learn a whole series of communication skills in order to overcome this illusion. That is another vital step in this larger process: learning to

---

[7] Hummingbird Community in northern New Mexico is a model of the new type of organism that is emerging at this time. This group is modeling conscious evolution and the practices of Co-Creation in their everyday lives and businesses. Go to www.hummingbirdccw.com for additional information.

listen and to cooperate with one another - taking full self-responsibility for one's own thoughts, feelings and behavior. The following agreements, which have been developed and shared widely for over 30 years, form a basis for building group trust and coherence.

The Co-Creator's Agreements[8]

As a group rests in the resonant field of love and trust, an opening in their collective consciousness naturally occurs. Individuals gain the capacity of tuning into higher patterns of creation. Wisdom comes forth as each person gains access to personal insights and revelations. It is as though higher mind, a higher level of thinking, emerges in this "we-space" - calling forth the genius of the group.

Another aspect of this process is the discovery of each member's life purpose, which is perhaps the most self-rewarding gift a person can ever receive. The unearthing of one's purpose brings meaning, value and a deep sense of fulfillment. It is a fundamental step in the process of becoming a true Co-Creator and contributing to the birth of a new society.

Once individuals discover their deeper calling in life, they are drawn to others who are aligned with their values, vision, and mission so that the unique purpose of each person can be actualized. This aspect of the process, called shared purpose, connects Co-Creators with one another in the small group or team and is a microcosm of the larger process of connection that can transform society at large by engendering greater complexity and fostering higher consciousness and an expanded sense of freedom!

---

[8] These agreements are taken from *The Co-Creator's Handbook* by Carolyn Anderson with Katharine Roske. They have been adapted from The Geneva Group Agreements, Boulder, CO. Go to www.thecocreatorshandbook.com for a free copy.

Co-Creative practices that guide us toward self-governance and new forms of inspired decision-making allow for right action to be revealed in the collective resonant field. The group moves beyond consensus decision-making and aligns with the higher pattern of "what wants to happen." Synergistic decision-making is not a process of voting, controlling, or convincing others to see things a certain way. It involves learning to listen deeply from within and shifting thinking from "I" to "We." This is "seventh generation" decision-making that takes into account the health of the system as a whole, the well-being of all species and the Earth itself - for centuries to come. The Core Group Process culminates in the practice of giving back to society and serving others.

Individuals experience that they gain greater capacities by consciously connecting with other Co-Creators. It is this massive connectivity of evolved humans worldwide, facilitated by the internet and social media that brings the promise of whole systems' transformation.

The Winds of Change Are Blowing

Right now humanity is living through one of the major transformations in human consciousness that has ever occurred on this planet. By learning and living the practices of Co-Creation, individuals and groups can participate in one of the greatest adventures that the human race has ever faced: the transformation of society and birth of a new world based on the values of love, trust, justice, beauty, equality and empathy for all. Large numbers of people are taking a leap in consciousness, claiming a new identity, and expressing greater creativity and deeper love. They are stepping across a threshold and contributing to the birth of a new world.

The change that changes everything is this transformation of consciousness, the shift from separation and fear to unity and love, the mass awakening to our true nature as divine beings, the realization that everything is connected to everything else and that we are the directors of our destiny. Our promise and our challenge is that our fate is tied to one another and to our mutual awakening! As true social pioneers, we are following our inner guidance, claiming a new empowered identity, giving our unique gifts, and creating a new world. We know that we are about to take a great leap and we are ready!

--

To contact Carolyn:

carolyn@livingcocreation.com

www.livingcocreation.com

Anita Agers Brooks

Anita Brooks motivates others to dynamic break-throughs, blending mind, heart, and spirit, as an inspirational coach, international speaker, and award-winning author. Her latest book, *Getting Through What You Can't Get Over,* and *First Hired, Last Fired - How to Become Irreplaceable in Any Job Market,* are currently available at all major bookstores, Amazon, plus other online retailers.

Anita fulfills her mission to help 21st century women and men make fresh starts with fresh faith by sharing what she's learned through experience, interviews, and research. She's energized by overcoming adversity, work with integrity, healthy relationships, identity issues, and abundant living. Anita inspires audiences all over the world to believe as she does - in business, as in life and love, it's never too late!

Anita's favorite pastime is watching sunsets with her husband of over 30 years, while they laugh and dip their toes in the water. Her favorite passion is inspiring others to take life's battles, and transform them into victories.

The Power of A Name Change

By Anita Agers Brooks

Call Me Courageous

By September 23, 2010, I'd endured a wave of tsunami-like tragedies. Sometimes, I felt like I couldn't catch my breath. But when you survive enough adversity and a new wave hits, the benefit of past experience guides you past the emotional debris and keeps the undertow from pulling you under.

You can look up to the heavens and say, "Lord, I don't know how you're going to get me through this, but you helped me in the past and I'll trust you to do it now."

I needed this, when on September 23rd, I received shocking news. A secret revelation that sent me swimming toward the truth of my identity. At forty-six years old, I did not expect to discover my dad is not my biological father.

My world immediately began to spin out of control. Everything I believed to be true about my life came into question. Things I accepted as fact no longer made sense. It felt like solid earth was jerked from beneath my feet. Everything good around me was swamped by this seismic news. For me, it was a pervasive tremor - my life would never be the same.

However, early on, because of what I'd learned previously, I made a choice. Unrelated to my emotional state, in spite of my feelings, I would exercise faith in the face of my fears.

I refused to call myself an accident. I decided I exist on purpose, with purpose, to fulfill a purpose. My Father knitted me in my mother's womb, and I focused on His image. I did not allow this change in my life to define me - I embraced it as a catalyst and gave myself a new name. I christened myself Courageous, but not because I felt that way.

I realized, you can't experience courage without fear first. So if you feel afraid, it's the best time to exercise bravery.

This makes me think of you. What's swirling in your life?

Whatever it is, refuse to go under - there's power in rebirth. Rename yourself Courageous.

Call Me Worthy

"It's okay to be alive." Not everyone gets this statement.

Until you do, old fears, subconscious beliefs, habits, and self-destructive behaviors can keep you imprisoned behind an invisible force shield of shame. I used to believe lies of debilitating self-worth, until I discovered the power in a name change. Labels matter, but we do not have to accept those relegated to us, we can choose positive portraits, reinforcing our intended destinies. We are meant for more - *you* are meant for more.

Don't let anything hold you back - your past, your emotions, not even your present conditions. Give yourself permission to be your best self and give yourself more.

Relabel yourself Worthy.

Call Me Talented

I grew up in a family of artists. Painters and sketchers with award-winning gifts. Then there was me. I spent years struggling to draw stick people - I never did perfect the craft. I did however, perfect the art of beating myself up. I concentrated so much energy on what I couldn't do, that I missed what I could.

Some people are conditioned by voices berating them over years and decades for perceived flaws and weaknesses. Often-times, much verbal abuse comes from our own internal dialogue. We tell ourselves, "You'll never measure up. Why can't you do things like, So-and-So? You're lazy. Stupid. Useless. Doomed."

We lie to ourselves, believing the misinformation fed into our brains by hurting people who hurt other people. We fall prey to seeing ourselves only through the lens of lack.

Focusing on what we can't, versus building on what we can.

As a Certified Personality Trainer and Inspirational Business/Life Coach, I help people understand the truth - we all have strengths and weaknesses. Comparisons are foolish, we need the balance of diversity to lead us to peaceful, productive, and prosperous lives. Creativity comes from pooling our resources, and we all have something to give. Including you.

In my case, I wasted a lot of years fretting because I couldn't draw, when I could have used that time to refine my own natural talent for painting pictures with words. Thankfully, I halted the lie saying, "You have no gifts."

I reinvested my energy into unearthing my own inherent skills. They were there all along, underneath my nose, things that came so easily I took them for granted. I didn't see them as anything special, assuming everyone could string sentences. I thought all people envisioned tactical and strategic outcomes when a problem arose. It surprised me to find others weren't intrigued by digging up lessons and sharing them through stories.

Once I became aware of the truth of my abilities, I made another change. With intentionality, I altered my inner dialogue. You can do it too.

One moment at a time, one day after another, allowing positive self-talk to transform you over weeks that stretch into months and years, you can identify and accept your gifts. Search for those things you can do with little effort. Pay attention to the small things others ask you to help with. Stop focusing on what you can't - pursue what you can.

Change your name to Talented.

Call Me Teachable

I was at my first writer's conference. The acquisitions publisher smiled at me, "This is a very relevant concept. I'd like to see a proposal on your idea." My spirits soared.

But just as quickly, my emotions plummeted. I realized I didn't know how. I'd drafted many a business proposal, I'd helped numerous clients create sellable loan proposals for banks, but as of that date, I'd never written a book proposal.

At this same conference, a session speaker shared a discouraging statistic, "Only 1% of aspiring authors ever succeed in getting published and paid."

Had I wasted my time and money on the investment to come here?

But then the session speaker continued, "Because most aspiring writers give up and quit when things get hard. You should know, becoming a published author is very difficult, unless you pay someone to print your book, versus them paying you."

In that moment, I realized I faced a crossroad. Would I pack up my dreams, give up, and go home? Or would I resolve to become one of the one? To persist with tenacity and determination until I succeeded in becoming one of the 1% of writers who achieved? Whose vision became reality?

I chose the latter - but I knew, I couldn't proceed half-cocked, or else, my aspirations would end up in a lifeless heap of dead dreams. Like 99% of those who once allowed themselves to set their hearts on something great, only to let rejection kill their call.

I used a secret weapon. And it lead to the publication of *First Hired, Last Fired - How to Become Irreplaceable in Any Job Market.* The book that launched my success as a published author.

I resolved to maintain a teachable spirit. I first set a goal to read 100 books on the craft and business of writing. It took me eighteen months. But when I finished, I had studied, practiced, and refined, to the point of having two book proposals completed. When I met the woman who would sign me to my literary agency, I *just so happened,* to have these proposals ready when she asked what I was working on.

When professionals made suggestions for improvement on my work, I didn't disregard their advice, but weighed it thoughtfully against other research and resources. I did my best to implement, having discovered that wisdom is the application of knowledge. I made it my mantra to listen twice as much as I spoke, realizing God gave me one mouth and two ears for a reason. While I learned, I gained favor as well as real-life schooling.

This is an education anyone can afford. You can decide in advance not to give up. You can set goals and attain knowledge. You can become a tenacious learner. You can listen twice as much as you speak and apply what you're taught. You can become one of the one.

Make yourself Teachable.

Call Me Empowered

A real change in my professional life came several years ago when I took courage and started calling myself a writer and speaker. Professional coaching came later as a natural evolution of those early brave decisions. In empty and silent rooms I spoke out loud to myself, "You are a writer. You are a speaker. You are a coach."

When I first used those designations, it wasn't a lie, but I wasn't writing, speaking, and coaching for money. At that stage in my life, I was giving those services away.

Writing as a hobby, as well as helping others draft letters, proposals, and college papers. I spoke to groups as part of my day job for years. Word spread and other agencies called. I coached family, friends, and was referred to numerous individuals before I pursued certifications or charged a penny for my guidance.

Perhaps you're beginning to see a pattern here, sometimes our greatest gifts are so natural we take them for granted. We disregard our own value, and too often give precious things away. Don't get me wrong, there's a time and place for giving, I'm thankful for my generous gene. However, it's also appropriate to receive adequate compensation for highly prized investments in others.

So what name do you need to give yourself? Author, Painter, Dress-Suit Maker?

Whatever your dream, start daring to tag yourself by it. Privately at first. To an intimate circle of people you trust next. Until finally, one day, you go public. Infusing yourself with the gumption to make it real by saying it out loud to a crowd.

Tag yourself Empowered.

Call Me Targeted

There's a difference between an aspiration, a dream, and a goal.

An aspiration means we have a drive, compulsion, or ambition for something more than what we've currently attained. Often, it is an abstract desire. For instance, as a professional writer, at one time I aspired to get my work published. There was no clear vision, precise actions, or strategy outlined.

A dream is more concrete. We have a specific image in mind of what we want to achieve, where we want to go, or who we want to become. We have some detailed ideas of how to get there, but we don't have a timeline in place. We don't write it down. I could imagine a book with my name on it as the author, but had taken little action.

A goal is tied to tactical steps with a date stamp for completion. We envision what the final outcome will look like, solidify our intentions in writing, including identified actions that will take us to our desired destination.

When I created my goals as a writer, this is the condensed process I followed:

Daily Affirmations: "Today I will make a fresh start with fresh faith, learning from yesterday, imagining tomorrow, growing today." I wrote my affirmations down, and posted them on mirrors, my refrigerator, put them in my wallet, my car, and any other place I frequented.

Weekly Small-Sized Goals: Each week, I set four goals starting with a verb. I gave myself seven days to act.

1. Read one chapter from an inspiring book, or a magazine/website article that motivates me. I will highlight and/or write notes on those things that encourage me the most.

2. Take one action that scares me enough to cause me to catch my breath; research, study, practice something positive connected to my dreams.

3. Ask for an opportunity, (write an article query), or say yes to an offer at least once this week.

4. Create and/or maintain spreadsheets for tracking goal results.

Monthly Medium-Sized Goals:

1. Mark off completed goals and add new as needed.

2. Review my weekly goals, give myself a treat to celebrate my successes, and review detailed tactics to see where I can improve on lesser achievements.

3. Pursue and/or pay for professional edits of my writing, to nip poor habits early, and develop good habits in my practices.

4. Connect with at least three new industry professionals through social media, email, or conferences.

Yearly Triumph-Sized Goals:

1. Review misses and hits for previous year's goals, including the why behind the what.

2. Set new target goals for the coming year, including refreshers on priority - God, family, business.

3. Interview people formally and informally to discover their current needs at work and in their personal lives.

4. Research latest findings and insider insights related to current needs.

5. Write and submit a new book proposal to my agent for publication.

6. Update and create new speaking presentations for conferences and other events for the year.

7. Outline best solutions from my own life and coaching clients in order to share with new businesses, organizations, agencies, and individuals.

Get the idea? You can draw your future with brushstrokes today.

Paint yourself Targeted.

Call Me Doer

Without action, our aspirations, dreams, and goals are meaningless. In order to succeed, I must define myself as a doer - not a hearer, thinker, or talker only. Paraphrasing Ecclesiastes 5:5 in the Bible, I often remind myself and others, "It's better not to make a promise than to make one and break it."

Refining natural raw talent into something polished and more meaningful takes elbow grease. We can't shine without effort. Don't break promises - even those to yourself.

As a business coach, every leader I've worked with, when asked what they want from their management, employees and staff, express the same desires. Those team members who are doers. Who exhibit integrity at an intrinsic level, doing the same thing whether they believe anyone else can see or hear them or not.

In a culture looking out for number one, if you want to set yourself apart from the crowd, dare to be different. Don't just talk - do. People notice. If you want to achieve your goals, make your dreams come true, and live up to your aspirations, take action.

Define yourself as a Doer.

Call Me Grateful

"I don't know if you'll get your eyesight back."

These were not comforting words. And as I sat in a blinding white exam room, fluids coursing from both of my stinging, red-rimmed eyes, this was not what I wanted to hear from my ophthalmologist. Especially as an aspiring writer only two years into serious pursuit of my life-long dream.

After I met with his colleague, also clueless, I panicked. How could I make a living as a blind person? How would I navigate my own house? How could I help others when I couldn't help myself? How would I write?

Once home, I felt my way straight to my bedroom and following doctor's orders for bed rest, pulled the blankets up to my chin. Then I cried. And sobbed. And heaved some more. The pity-party I threw myself was in full tear-soaked swing.

A couple of hours later, sniffling and hiccupping, I began to review my life. The good. The bad. The tragedies. A pattern emerged.

I realized every difficult thing I'd experienced eventually transformed into something I could use to comfort, help, teach, or encourage others. The same circumstances I listed as adversity, over time, became something I listed as a blessing. The ashes of my pain became crowns of beauty.

In that moment, my perspective changed, though my circumstances were the same. I started looking for miracles in my problems. I considered new ways to do old things. I would be okay, whether I was able to see again or not.

Over the next few days, as people called or visited, I focused on thanks for the good things in my life, instead of dwelling on my fears. In those scary early days when I was blind, I discovered words have the power to harm or to heal. I was eventually diagnosed with a genetic eye disease, and though I deal with residual symptoms, my sight is restored.

Regardless of circumstances, what you speak can determine your emotional outcome. Expressing thanks can set you on the road to recovery. You can decide to be okay, whether you do or don't see. What you call yourself in the process can make all the difference. There's power in a name.

Crown yourself Grateful.

Call Me Triumphant

I recently met with a new coaching client who said, "I want to be more confident, but I don't know how." I've heard similar statements from countless women and men throughout the years - many in high-powered positions.

I asked this person a series of specific questions, helping them identify important missing elements critical to making confident decisions. At first, they referred to themselves through the lens of tragedy, versus believing in their ability to triumph. They called themselves failure instead of winner. They needed a reframe.

Painful challenges have taught me to reframe my own life. This is how I know, "In business, as in life and love - It's never too late for a fresh start with fresh faith."

Life may come at you like a tsunami, you may feel battered by debris and fear the suction of undertow. How you define yourself in the midst of the storm can determine where you land when waves calm. Remember, it doesn't seem like it when a wall of water reaches its full height, but water recedes as fast as it rises.

Reframe yourself Triumphant.

Tough times hit us all. When you see the swell of adversity approaching, when you feel powerless, arm yourself with a name change. These are the motivators with the power to heal, to help you ride any wave. Don't cower, stand.

You were made for more - call yourself Transformed.

You are Courageous

You are Worthy

You are Talented

You are Teachable

You are Empowered

You are Targeted

You are Doer

You are Grateful

You are Triumphant

To contact Anita:

You can connect with Anita on Facebook, YouTube, Pinterest, LinkedIn, or Twitter. Keep up with Anita's latest happenings at anitabrooks.com.

Email anita@anitabrooks.com to request information on having Anita speak or train at your next event.

Nansey Sinclaire

Although she created a six figure income for herself, raised her husband's business to the top of its field and devoted herself to learning at every opportunity, Nansey Sinclaire ultimately came to the realization that something was missing... the power, the money, and all the lovely things and experiences money could buy - were nice, thank you, but wasn't there something else...?

Co-author of *The Mysteries of a Woman, 1000 Tips for Teenagers*, and former Vancouver food critic columnist, this adventurous traveler has faced her serious fears head-on: unable to swim and terrified of being underwater, she acquired her open-water diving accreditation, walked on fire with Tony Robbins, and became an educational and motivational public speaker.

As an open-line radio show host and online tele-seminar leader, Nansey's exceptional people skills elicited thought-provoking interviews and discussions with over one hundred and thirty authors, self-development professionals and spiritual leaders.

Currently a mastermind facilitator, business owner and healthcare sensitivity trainer, Nansey is in the research phase of her 'big picture' project: a resort for children and families with disabilities.

There really WAS something else... Living a life that she loves!

Thank You, I Forgive You, it's All My Fault!

By Nansey Sinclaire

Being grateful was not the focus of my life in the beginning of 2009. In fact, I was so focused on what was not working, that I wasted hours documenting my unhappiness in my daily journals - mostly conclusive evidence of why I was so miserable in my second marriage.

The idea of failing in a second marriage wasn't a thought I savored, and my husband and I were unable to admit out loud that it wasn't working. It was beyond our capabilities at that time to do something constructive or proactive about our situation. Instead we let it spiral downward into a potpourri of wounded egos, hostile words, and idle threats.

A profound sadness hovered over us with no glimmer of hope in sight. Stuck in protecting ourselves emotionally, we were unable to reach beyond our fragile egos to take personal responsibility for our own contributions to the situation.

The Law of Attraction was working exceptionally well during that period of my life, unfortunately in reverse. My need to vent my anger, resentment, and frustration daily in my journals had not gone unnoticed by the Universe. As I wrote to affirm my reasons and my indignant right to be miserable, I was rewarded with more evidence to support my claims... creating the very situation that I was so disgruntled about.

The first time I got married, at the age of 23, I really had no idea why I was doing it. I recall thinking to myself, "I guess this is what I'm supposed to do." The decisions in my life were in large part a result of unconscious thinking. I made decisions based on perceived expectations about the people around me. In those moments, I was not acting responsibly relative to what I desired for my life. At no point had I sat down and laid out what I would like my life to look like. There were no goals or visions either immediate or long term, that I was inspired to move towards. I was reacting in the moment, not responding to what life was calling me to do.

Years later, when I chose to get married the second time, I felt more in control of my life and was far more aware of the choices and the decisions I was making; I believed they were positive, life-enhancing and supportive of the direction I wanted to go.

However, as time progressed, our marriage began to fall apart. The signs were all there although we wanted to ignore them: we slept in separate bedrooms, doing our utmost to ignore one another while attempting to live two separate lives under the same roof. We engaged with one another only when it seemed there was little other choice, and when we did, we fought most of the time.

My instinct told me what to do, however I wasn't able to trust my heart and do what was intuitively right for me. I was caught up in my head - allowing my thoughts to dictate my actions.

I wasn't aware at the time that we have approximately 90,000 thoughts a day running through our minds and for the most part, they're negative thoughts. Not only are they negative, we tend allow the same thought to repeat over and over. Eventually I came to understand the insidious power behind that action and the impact that negative thinking can have in a person's life, namely mine.

At the insistence of my girlfriend, my former husband and I both watched the movie The Secret - she claimed it would change my life. It was an "ah-ha" moment for me as I began to realize what I had been creating between us in our relationship. I was captivated by the idea of the Law of Attraction and I wanted to learn as much as I could. I began paying careful attention to MY thoughts and what was occurring in my life. My desire for peace was so strong that I was willing to do anything I could to change the current situation.

I began writing a gratitude list daily. I deliberately started looking for things about my husband that I could appreciate, including the times we were conflict free. I read... and read... personal development and empowerment material from the BIG GUNS. Books on how our mind, body and spirit are connected AND how our bodies manifest our inner emotions, thoughts and beliefs about ourselves. By looking at the way I'd been feeling - how overwhelmed, stressed and unhappy I was, and additionally, how the physical pain in my body was increasing with headaches, lower back and shoulder pain - I realized I was doing all of this to myself!

I was completely responsible for what I was creating in my life.

The discovery of the power of our thoughts was transformational for me. I had no idea that I was attracting more of what I hadn't wanted. Because I was spending so much time focusing on how unhappy I was, the Law of Attraction had been invoked... and I had no idea.

Studying all the material I could get my hands on was beginning to change me, and as I changed, I never went back to the 'old me.' Unlike 'Transformers,' that can be changed and then moved back to their original form, I was not interested in ever returning to my previous condition of miserable and unhappy - I was committed to positive powerful change that would move my life forward.

However, our responses to the movie were very different. With my change came his resistance to who I was becoming, and the gap between us widened even more. We were both seeking something significant that would radically change our present circumstance. My journey took me on an inward trek. He didn't understand the direction I took, which fueled even more angst towards me.

Eventually, a potentially explosive exchange occurred, during which I made the decision to contact the police. Change was made in that moment and there was no turning back.

My decision to get out of the marriage had not come with a plan, however once my husband had been removed from the house, I felt an immediate sense of relief. I had been emotionally, mentally and physically drained by all the conflict and now the energy in the house changed drastically. I felt happier, more peaceful and particularly grateful. Having him leave the house was worth all the unknowns that were about to come my way. I had searched for a way to stop the craziness and finally, it had ground to a halt.

Within a week, I received an email inviting me to a three day self-development conference in San Diego with some of the best speakers and leaders in the field. Intuitively, I followed the calling without any idea of what to expect or whether I could afford to attend, I just knew that I was being called to say YES to the opportunity.

Three weeks later, when a taxi dropped me at the convention center, I claimed a seat in the front row, placed my suitcase under the chair and sat back to learn, as speaker after speaker stood on the stage and shared their personal 'victim-to-victor' story.

I listened attentively, wrote copious notes, and purchased numerous books and coaching programs from the back of the room. I believe I actually signed up for everything!

That began a full time study of personal development and empowerment from the best known names in the field: online, audio, video, books, CD's, tele-seminars, PDF reports, and more. I became a sponge, soaking up every tidbit of information, doing every exercise and reading every website give-away meant to improve our lives. Friends affectionately dubbed me a 'seminar junkie.' I had become like Phoenix Rising, my head facing the sky and my wings ready for flight: I had experienced the possibility of change and was salivating for more.

The changes began incrementally at first. I focused on things that made me happy and things I was grateful for.

I began looking forward to the future and deciding what kind of life would I like to have. I looked at my current life and began wondering, "What things would I like to experience in the next five years, ten years, and what sort of legacy would I like to leave as a celebration of my time on the planet?"

I decided to create my life *by design* as opposed to it just unfolding without any specific input. I began *doing to life* instead of allowing life to happen to me.

My writing took on a whole new meaning. Although in the past I had spent a lot of time complaining in my journal about the misery of my relationship, I had also spent time in 'general curiosity' about life.

Now I was getting even more curious, "Who am I now? Why and how have I attracted these situations that have made me so unhappy?" What were my thoughts and what had prompted them?

Our conditioned thinking comes from the many experiences we've had in our past. Things that we heard as young children get stuck in our minds and become our truth. We begin to believe the negative things, either about ourselves directly or about how we can expect to be treated as we grow up. These thoughts become ingrained in our minds and we tend to believe that they're true. They become the program running in the back of our minds and we're not even aware that it's occurring.

I wondered where I had developed many of the beliefs I had about myself and life in general, unaware until then how negative many of them were: beliefs around marriage, men, women, my strengths and weaknesses, my self-worth, and also about money and relationships.

What valuable insight I gained! To be able to understand why over the years, I'd attracted relationships that were unhealthy or unfulfilling. I was attracting men to my life that reflected the feelings I had about myself, my value and my self-worth!

I noticed patterns in my beliefs and began connecting dots about relationships with men that had been negative, hurtful and abusive. I also starting exploring thoughts, feelings and emotions that I had about being adopted as a newborn from Argentina.

As I continued making the connections, I noticed where my feelings of unworthiness had come from. The theme of abandonment had become apparent. All of these thoughts, feelings and emotions had been tucked away, deep in my subconscious and I was unaware that they even existed!

Now that I had discovered them, the next step was to learn: what to do with them, how to process, heal and surrender them so that I could move forward and experience the complete inner peace that I was seeking so desperately. I committed to doing 'the work.'

If I had created my experiences by default, then I wanted to know why. When I discovered how much pain, sadness and feelings of loss were beneath the surface, I pushed myself to go through the processes that I needed to - in order to affect healing, understanding, acceptance and forgiveness.

- I committed to becoming compassionate and loving towards myself.

- I allowed myself the permission to sit, raw with my emotions, and feel all of the emotional pain that came with it.

- I allowed myself to feel the anger, sadness, and even the shame that surfaced when I gave myself permission to wallow in the depths of my emotions.

Surprisingly, my greatest joy transpired on the other side of that experience.

Through various exercises, I began an intensive process of forgiveness for every possible transgression that had brought up a negative emotional response in my body. I was determined to let go of all the painful memories, emotions and energy that were still tightly attached to my definition of who I was.

Once I began to realize how powerful my thoughts were, I became devoutly vigilant about them. By being mindful of my conscious thoughts, I became committed to replacing the negative, destructive thoughts I was having at an unconscious level.

My first step was to become personally responsible for everything that was occurring in my life. If I was unhappy there was no one to blame but myself; I had the opportunity to choose the thoughts I wanted to embrace and the decisions I wanted to make. No one held a gun to my head - if I wasn't happy then I needed to do something about it: take action, not complain about what wasn't working.

Shifting into personal responsibility allowed me to get real with my thoughts, feelings and emotions. Having a better understanding of how so many negative thoughts and beliefs had developed, I was able to begin replacing the negative thoughts with empowering thoughts and to start the process of forgiveness: towards myself and to others who I felt had harmed or hurt me over the years. I was able to let go of the painful emotional attachment to experiences that I had repressed and that were profoundly affecting my self-image, confidence and self-esteem.

The healing process very intense and truly life changing. Every time I surrendered, healed and let go of another layer of self-doubt, fear or disbelief, the result was a raised level of esteem and increased output of positive vibrations. The more I love and accept who I am, the more I am able to show up as a compassionate, loving and forgiving human being towards others.

Our life's journey is to bring us to the point of valuing what's important. Unconscious patterns of thinking, and the inability to take full responsibility for our thoughts, choices and actions, contribute to our feelings of un-fulfillment, frustration and unhappiness. The steps to change involve:

- recognizing what we're thinking
- understanding how our thinking impacts our experience
- deciding if we wish to continue the experience, and, if not,
- committing to positive powerful change by changing our thoughts

Claiming personal responsibility for my entire life: choices, thoughts, decisions and actions, was MY starting point. Forgiving myself and others for the thoughts, emotions and negative beliefs that had been harboring, was the next step. I followed up with a commitment to focus on gratitude and what was working in my life.

Change does happen in a moment. The minute we decide that we want something different, better, or more, we have the ability to create it - it all starts with our thoughts. By focusing on our contribution to what's occurring, and then focusing on what we have to be grateful for, we are beginning positive and meaningful change. You have it within you to create the experience of your lifetime

What things in your life would you like to change? Have you given thought to what is working well, or perhaps, to what could use improvement? Is it possible that there is room for improvement in everyone's life?

One of the things I have become aware of is how often people are caught up in the familiar. I believe it's easy to take things for granted, not realizing that we're on autopilot instead of stepping outside our comfort zone to something far more empowering. Most individuals operate from a conditioned state of thinking, reacting and responding. We are, for the most part, programmed by experiences of our past. Impacted by the manner in which we were brought up, we operate on belief systems that we were taught as youngsters. When we operate from our subconscious mind instead of our conscious mind, we do not exercise control in our life. We give away our power.

We give away the opportunity to create powerful interactions, conversations and choices that could impact our lives in a meaningful way.

Recently I was in a coffee shop and couldn't help but overhear a conversation next to me, entirely about a specific food item that this woman was searching for at a couple of different grocery stores. She went into great detail about her search for the item and then her dismay at the cost of the item once she located it. What caught my attention was how much time, effort and energy she put into the conversation and how agitated and annoyed she became the more she talked about it!

At the time, I was reading a personal empowerment book and thought about the differences in our energy in that moment. I was being uplifted by inspirational thoughts and experiences while this woman was lowering her enthusiasm for the day by focusing on how difficult it was to locate the item. Of course, after the initial focus on the grocery item itself, the conversation lengthened to include all the other negative aspects of the grocery store in general. It was a downward spiral.

As cliché as it sounds, life is short. Our choices in life are infinite. Our time on earth is not. Time truly is precious. We all have the opportunity to deliberately create our own experience. Given a choice to empower ourselves through our thoughts or disempower ourselves the same way, I'm sure most of us would pick the obvious.

I spent a number of years choosing disempowering thoughts relative to my relationship before deciding that my life was far more valuable than the unhappiness I was creating. My wish is for YOU: to seize the opportunity and embrace the notion of taking complete responsibility for your life. Be mindful of YOUR thoughts: do they support or deplete your life? Are you enacting the law of attraction for your 'highest good' or are you attracting more of what you don't want?

If you are interested, OR even better, committed to making a positive change in your life, the three aspects of gratitude, forgiveness and responsibility-for-self are most certainly the keys to shifting your life in the right direction. You can begin immediately... just by thinking.

To contact Nansey:

www.nanseysinclaire.com:

nanseysinclaire@gmail.com

(604) 841-3134

Kevin Allen

Kevin Allen has spent the last 30 years in the network marketing industry where he has successfully filled the roles of VP of Sales, President & CEO and Owner, all on multiple occasions. He is highly sought after as a public speaker and trainer on the largest stages in the world. Kevin has performed on the national stage as a singer and actor as well. His charisma and presence make him one of the best there is, every time he takes the stage. Kevin's ability to customize presentations for any specific audience is a rare trait in the industry. Whomever he speaks to, the audience feels like his words are being spoken for the very first time for their special situation.

Kevin loves personal empowerment and knowledge cultivation and finds personal gratification in taking his audiences, whether one or thousands, to a new level of self-awareness and personal ability realization. Kevin is bilingual in English and Spanish and has also spoken through interpreters in dozens of other countries, having toured extensively in Asia.

Kevin is married to his lovely wife Robin and they share 7 children and 20 grandchildren. They reside in Queen Creek, Arizona.

The Watermelon Sale

By Kevin Allen

In life, you can never know where your greatest lessons will come from or when they will arrive. They seldom happen when you seek them. Lessons come, as we all know, when the student is ready. The Universe's role in the timing of these moments is widely disputed; nonetheless, there seems to be something more than happenstance involved in the great learning moments of our lives. Who would ever imagine that possibly the greatest lesson in sales training I would ever receive would be as a twelve-year-old Boy Scout at a fundraising event? The sale was to raise money for a new quartermaster chuck box that would carry the cooking gear and serving gear for our entire scout troop. We knew the price would be high because we wanted the best of the best. We were a seasoned group of little salesmen since our scoutmaster believed in sales as an art form.

Our previous sales were small potatoes compared to the event we faced this day. We had sold our share of family dinner tickets (usually spaghetti for the best profit margins), and we had sold magazine subscriptions. We had sold yard and home clean-up services, and we had hoed our share of weed-filled gardens. One challenging sale was lightbulbs. We walked into the scout room to find boxes and boxes of lightbulbs, every wattage and every size imaginable. I learned some lessons that night, the biggest one being that I could have done much better by carrying an order book for the first hour and returning to deliver bulbs later, thus offering everyone every possible combination of bulbs. By carrying what I thought everyone would want, frosted 100 watt bulbs, I missed a lot of sales. Apparently 60 watt clear bulbs were the favorite. But I later saw how I could have sold everyone everything he or she wanted. That was a great lesson too.

Today's sale, the sale with life's greatest sales lesson, was happening on a hot summer day in the middle of the Great Sonoran Desert, and the sale's object was a delicacy of the region; 4th of July Klondike watermelons brought up from just across the Mexico border.

By the time we gathered at Scoutmaster Conrad's house at 9:00 a.m. that Saturday morning in Phoenix, Arizona, in early July, the temperature had already found the century mark. As scouts in Conrad's troop, you found us all, as always, in full Boy Scouts of America official uniforms. As I remember, about twenty-two boys showed up for this sale; after all, these activities were unofficially mandatory.

Most of the boys had already given this sale some thought before that morning. The top prize for selling the most watermelons was an official scout hatchet. Not the lightweight version, but the heavy duty, bright, red-headed hatchet with an ash handle just like baseball bats were carved from. The hatchet came with a leather holster that had two belt slots in it for wearing when hiking. Now that's a prize!

The scout motto of "Be prepared" was manifested by young scouts showing up with red wagons, some pulled on foot and some being wildly towed behind a stingray bicycle. Others who were paperboys or had a paperboy in their family showed up on a Schwinn Paperboy Special with canvas paper bags on the handlebars and some with wire baskets in the back. A few showed up with their backpacks ready to fill with melons. It was quite a sight and immediately obvious that I was not the only scout there that day who had his eye on that hatchet. This would be a fight to the finish. My vehicle of choice was multi-faceted. I would hit the closest houses in the neighborhood on foot with a wagon first thing, and then work my way out farther, switching to my bike when the distance became an issue.

When we arrived at Conrad's house, the setting was magical. Oh, it was hot, but imagine our eyes when we saw one of the mulberry trees in Conrad's front yard with what seemed to be a pile of snow beneath its green branches. It was snow. Where we lived, it never snowed, but there on the ground in the heat of the summer, it was amazing to behold. The melons had been delivered the night before, a couple of hundred of them at least. Okay, maybe just a hundred. The melons had been carefully stacked at the foot of the tree where shade would be afforded if the sale made it into the noon hour, which was certainly unlikely. Using the tree as a stacking post, the melons were built up into a shiny green pyramid, and then early that morning, the magic happened. Conrad called in the local ice house with a truck mounted machine none of us ever dreamed existed - a snow-making machine. The snow was sprayed and layered on top of the melons, and now a few hours later, the ice cold watermelons were ready to be sold to a waiting Arizona summer's clientele. Many of us were awed by the sight. This was a bigger deal than any sale before, to be sure. An overwhelming excitement had every boy nervous with anticipation. This was the big time. Rules were shared, pricing clarified, the starting gun sounded, and the competition was on.

The melons averaged twenty-plus pounds each, and no kid was totally prepared for the challenges we faced that morning. I planned on taking six or eight melons in the little wagon on my first load but found instead that only two fit. Putting a watermelon in each side of a paper delivery bag made it impossible to steer the bicycle. Oh, you could turn the wheel easily enough, but the momentum of forty pounds in your bags would flip the whole bike around. Watching the kids try to ride their bicycles with melons in the bags was pretty funny, but it represented a problem for part of my plan as well. The wire baskets were of no value since no melon would fit into the narrow baskets made specifically for daily newspapers folded in quarters. For the first time ever, we veteran paperboys noticed that the wire baskets had wires ending in blunted off but otherwise sharp edges that quickly penetrated the beautiful green shells of the melons, almost disfiguring the beauties. The best choice quickly emerged as the "grab a melon and run" tactic where you might make it to an "easy house" while a competing scout was trying to get his load figured out. It was agreed that we would meet back at the scoutmaster's house at high noon to count the proceeds and announce the winner.

"Easy house" is a term all kids are fully aware of. It's not just a scout thing. It's about the person living in the house. An easy house might be a local church leader who will thoughtfully support any and every youth activity ever offered. It might be a relative. But the easy house we all sprinted for first was the little old lady who lived in the second house around the corner. She was a lady whom every kid knew. If you walked down her street on your way home from school, she would often wait outside to say hello and even offer you an apple or an orange to eat on your way. But her claim to fame, her crowning glory, happened each year at Halloween when this wonderful lady would hand out FULL SIZE candy bars. No kidding. She handed out full size *3 Musketeers* or *Snickers* or even a *Baby Ruth* or *Big Hunk*. Every kid loved her, and there was nothing she wouldn't buy from a smiling Boy Scout in uniform. I got there first - only she wasn't home. Sadly, she did return later and another scout happened along in time to help her unload her groceries. That led to an obvious watermelon sell. Like shooting fish in a barrel.

Scouts headed out in every direction and the snow pile was disturbed significantly. A couple of boys lingered behind, searching through the snow pile for the perfect melons. I later discovered that a few special melons were pulled out and hidden in the ivy growing on the shady side of the scoutmaster's home; very special melons that boys would return to sell when their others ran out. Conrad might have even known of this scheme since he was usually willing to allow boys their creative freedom as long as nobody cheated. The Watermelon Sale was underway and it appeared that it would be a speedy competition.

The picture at noon, however, was anything but what we had expected. Laying in the shade of the mulberry trees were thirteen scouts and what appeared to be more melons than when we had started. Nine boys had given up and gone home. The rest of us were there, as ordered, to check in at the close of the sale, but this sale was obviously far from over. The stories we told each other as we lay there were horrific! Even tried and true perfect past customers had turned us down. "The price is too high," or "They can't be ripe yet this season," or even blunt responses like "No thanks," were commonplace. This watermelon sale was a bust, and it was clear from the first or second house. Conrad had made a bad choice this time. (None of us acknowledged at that particular point that we had selected the product and voted on it as a troop.) We were in this state of co-misery and complaining when Conrad walked out of the house.

"What's going on boys?" he asked.

"Nobody wants to buy our watermelons," came the response.

"So are you finished then? Do you give up?" he queried.

"Yes," came the unanimous reply.

"All right then, no sense in letting these beautiful watermelons go to waste."

What Conrad did next none of us will ever forget. He walked over to the pile of stacked melons, which had only a few handfuls of snow remaining deep in the pile, and carefully extracted a perfect Klondike. None of us had seen that melon I guess, but now it loomed larger than life. Then he walked out to the curb to perform an act any surgeon would have respected as pure artistry. He bent over, and at the edge of the curb, he held the watermelon end to end, and with one smooth motion like the cracking of an egg, he cracked open the watermelon. It popped open like it was about to explode, and it made a sound like a pine tree being felled in the forest. Every scout was in awe. Then with equal skill, he used his bare hand to scoop the heart out of the melon and moved it to his mouth. We watched as the deep red juice squirted from both sides of his over-filled mouth and ran down his cheeks and off the tip of his chin. We were hot and exhausted and thirsty and, well, you get the picture. Conrad went through the flesh of that melon in mere seconds as we watched in wonderment. Then he wiped his mouth with his shirt sleeve.

"Well," he said, "no sense letting them all go to waste. Might as well help yourselves."

I'm only guessing, but I think it took less than fifteen minutes for each of us to attempt that same melon-busting technique and to fill ourselves with tasty goodness. Let it be well noted that nothing quenches and satisfies on a 110 degree day like an ice cold, perfectly ripened watermelon. Thirteen boys now lay belly up in the sunshine on a cool green lawn, stomachs each swollen with delight. This was summer heaven. Conrad had disappeared after his demonstration, but he now reemerged from the house.

"What did you think?" he asked.

Ooohhs and aaaahhs were offered as a response.

"Great melons, don't you think?"

More groans.

"Think your folks would like one?"

"Sure, yeah, absolutely!" we all chimed.

"All right then; here's what I want you all to do. Each of you take a melon to your mom or dad. Get them in the kitchen and use the side of the kitchen counter to pop open the watermelon. With a fork, I want you to cut a single bite out of the center of the melon, called "the heart." Give that bite to one of your parents to eat. After they sample the watermelon, tell them they can have the rest of it for just four dollars. Then come back and report."

This was exciting, and we were off at a dead run to share the greatest watermelons in the history of the world with our families.

By two o'clock that afternoon, every watermelon had been sold, and one very happy Boy Scout was awarded a shiny new hatchet. The scoutmaster's lesson that day, and something that cannot be considered anything less than a paradigm shift for the lot of us, had brought a successful ending to the Watermelon Sale. The principles I learned at the Watermelon Sale have shaped my life. I doubt that all the other scouts were impacted the same way or they studied the lessons they had learned that day as I did. But I loved selling! I loved the mechanics of selling and the disciplines and absolutes of mastering the skill set needed to earn a significant income for my entire life as a salesman. The visual image of seeing the heart cut out of a watermelon and the red juice dripping down the scoutmaster's chin that day has shaped many sales presentations in my life. As I write these words today, I can feel the excessive heat of that July, Arizona day. I can feel the coolness of being near that pile of man-made snow that covered the melons. I can see the explosion of red and hear the "crack" as Conrad popped open that first Klondike. I can see the faces of a dozen families as I shared the heart of a watermelon with them that afternoon. And I can feel the weight of that beautiful hatchet in my young hand as it was awarded to me for selling more melons than any other boy. For as long as I was in Boy Scouts, I had that hatchet, and for every day since then, I have had the lessons of how I won it.

There are as many ways to approach selling as there are people. I suppose I have used every technique through the years, but nothing compares with the "share the heart first" method. Of course, there is one huge requirement for this strategy. There must be a heart, and you must identify it.

Every salesperson has found him or herself at some point being trained on the technique of selling "features and benefits." It's pretty much exactly what it sounds like. You list the features and benefits of your product, the buyer sees the need, and the sale is completed. The heart is much, much more. The heart is what they cannot live without. What is the main benefit of your product? What above all else makes your product unique and desirable? If it's two things, then you're talking features or benefits, not the heart. There is only one heart, and once you identify it, you can sell it with great success.

The magic is two-fold. Step one is to share the heart, but step two is also important: "the take away." It's one thing to see the heart of a product, to desire it, to taste it, but only when the fear of losing that thing is present does the emotional rush say, *"I want this now, and you are not taking it from me."* Desire was created by sharing the heart of the watermelon with potential buyers, but the sale didn't happen until you got ready to take that melon and leave with it. The thought of losing that flavor after only one good bite was just too much to bear.

And so it was that as a twelve-year-old Boy Scout I learned a sales lesson that has put me at the top of my sales class for most of my life. To be successful, whether offering a product, a service, a business opportunity, or even a partnership, one need only identify and share the heart first, capturing the essence, the feeling, the flavor, the vision. After that, a willingness to take it all away, if it isn't appreciated at the same level you envision it, will, with little exception, end in a sale. Don't spend time on features and benefits. This world has lost its attention span for such discussions. Share the heart first, the whole heart, and watch your results rise at a level you cannot even imagine. And make no mistake; I've offered you the heart of what I have to give.

To contact Kevin:

(480) 242-2044

www.kevinallenspeaks.com

www.mlmman.com

www.facebook.com/mlmkevin

www.facebook.com/makingitinmlm

Julie Anderson

Julie Brain Lady Anderson is a dynamic and engaging international public speaker; business, communication, and relationship consultant; as well as a published author. Her fun and interactive presentations make the technical science behind psychology interesting and understandable. When Julie speaks, she captivates listeners with her natural, down-to-earth, and always energetic style. For more than 15 years, she has been igniting her audiences to fire up their brains. Her keynotes and workshops inspire positive changes in the relationships of all in attendance. The information she shares will help those who hear to accelerate their success in life and business through discovery of their natural gifts.

Julie has been interviewed on several radio stations including the ABC network, and made numerous television appearances. She studied Natural Health, Psychology, Human Resource Development and Psychoneuroimmunology at Clayton College. She is a 3 time attendee of Realizations Inc. / Success Resources International's Brain and Innate Giftedness program. She has also received CEC's in the field of Depression, Anxiety Disorders and Brain Function. She has done extensive research in the areas of Personality Types, Brain Function and Anatomy, Brain Health, and the Brain Personality Connection.

Change Your Mind - Step Into Your Power

By Julie 'Brain Lady' Anderson

What do you think of when you hear the term, "Change Your Mind?" Most people say it's deciding one thing now and later changing your decision. For example, you may want hamburgers for dinner but later opt for tacos. However, it can be more powerful than that; creating life-changing results. This chapter will show you why it's so important to "Change Your Mind!" and how to successfully make that change.

Most individuals never truly "Step Into Their Power." People spend most of their lives hiding their innate gifts; concealing their natural brain strengths. They spend large amounts of energy to work on so-called "weaknesses." Striving to achieve this can be extremely exhausting and depressing. Why? Because they're fighting against nature, trying to change what is encoded in their DNA. They'll spend massive amounts of brain energy to force a process that simply will not happen, resulting in negative emotions. Research shows there is a huge connection between thoughts, brain chemistry, and health.

Advancements in technology now allow researchers to take a large step forward in the field of neuroscience, seeing the brain as never before. A *huge* benefit of this research is that experts can now understand how the biochemical makeup of the brain effects who we are and why we do things the way we do; why some things come easily while others are difficult. This chapter will help you to become familiar with what I term the Brain Personality Connection (BPC). I'll also explain: why most struggle with being completely comfortable with their own BPC; how this can have negative effects on their health; and how you can take positive steps to "Change Your Mind and Step Into Your Power."

What is the Brain Personality Connection?

Dr. John J. Ratey, an expert in brain function, states: "A better understanding of how the brain works will give us a better way to get a handle on who we are." So gaining a clear picture of *your* BPC will help *you* to understand yourself and others better. Let me start to paint the picture of what the BPC looks like.

The BPC is made up of five main factors: Introversion/Extroversion level, Sensory Modality, Gender, Brain Quadrant Dominance, and Nurture. This is so much more than simply fascinating information. Gaining a clear picture of your own BPC will have life-changing results. But how can understanding your own brain gifts lead you to more success? Will gaining this scientific picture of your BPC actually improve not only your life and relationships but also your very health? If so, how is it that you "Change Your Mind!" to match your natural gifts? Before we can answer those questions, let's look at the science behind psychology.

The Science

Four of the five factors of your BPC are connected to your DNA. Each factor represents a different facet of your personality and will show up in its own way. Once they overlay on top of each other, they create the complex being that you are. The beauty is in the way you see the *gift* or *strength* connected to each facet. Always accentuate the positive!

First, the concept of Introversion/Extroversion. This became most popular with the research done by Carl Jung. This factor continues to be a prominent key in most personality tests, but it's only one of the five factors that I feel are crucial in understanding yourself and achieving your personal best. Most people will describe the difference between introversion and extroversion as being shy verses outspoken. However, we're looking at the *science;* this is the amount of external stimulus your brain needs to perform at its peak - where it's the happiest. This level is managed by the Reticular Activating System in your brain. It's science; not something you can simply change with a wish.

The Introvert's brain is naturally wide awake, needing little external stimulus to be happy. It looks at the world through a *huge* picture window; taking in plenty of information in one snapshot. Then it needs to retire to a low stimulus environment in order to process all the data; their brain can only handle so much stimulus before it's overwhelmed.

Introverts enter a room slowly and with caution. They'll generally gravitate towards one or two people; trying not to draw attention to themselves. They tend to automatically position themselves closest to the exit. This is their brain's way of providing itself with a quick escape if it gets overwhelmed.

This isn't anti-social behavior; it's the introvert's gift, taking in large amounts of information in small amounts of time. If you're an introvert, *change your mind* about the way you view your gifts. It's freeing to step into your power and use it to your advantage.

The Extroverts are just the opposite. They have a naturally sleepy brain. They crave high-stimulus environments in order for their brain to stay awake and perform at its peak. The extrovert's window to the world is more like a ships porthole. Since they don't get much information in one glance, they must continually look out of that window to keep gathering data.

Extroverts enter a room, throwing caution to the wind and moving quickly through it. They'll engage as many as possible, finding as much stimulus as they can. Most often, they'll position themselves in the middle of the room where their brain can receive exciting input from all directions, staying around the activity; keeping their brain happy.

While there is a real brain-based diagnosis for ADD/ADHD, beware of labels. They're not the same as the "gifts" connected to the extroverts. If you're an extrovert, you can perform well in situations where most cannot. Change your mind and *own* your extroversion as the gift is it.

It's important to consider the Ambiverts, since they're not discussed much when this topic comes up. Many people feel lost in their I/E identity, telling me that they have parts of both traits and have no idea where they fit. Very likely, they're an ambivert. Their brain is neither wide awake nor extremely sleepy. They can handle high-stimulus situations sometimes, but, other times, they want to be alone to think.

The introvert wants to have external stimulus only 10-20% of the time and 80-90% to themselves. The extrovert wants to spend 80-90% of their time with incoming stimulus and only 10-20% with none. While the ambivert is more of a 50/50 personality. They crave the interaction and stimulus half the time and want the other half to be quiet. You ambiverts can now breathe a sigh of relief. You've found your place!

The second factor is our Sensory Modality; aka, communication/learning style. This is how your brain processes information most efficiently and effectively. Unless sensory impaired, we use all of our senses to take in data. Research shows that each one of us tends to have one of the three preferences that works fastest. It's the path that incoming data hits the brain first and deepest. The three preferences are: auditory, visual, and kinesthetic.

Auditories, approximately 20% of the population, process information most efficiently when they hear it. It's interesting to note that reading is an auditory identifier. Your brain's auditory regions light up when you're reading. Sounds are important to this group, and they're easily irritated by what others may not notice. Words mean very much to this group, and they're the most hurt by harsh words said to them. They're gifted in listening and communicating through the spoken or written word.

Visuals, approximately 50% of the population, process information most efficiently when they see it. The way things look is very important to them. They'll almost always appear well put-together. They can notice the tiniest thing out of place: the piece of lint on your shirt or the picture on the wall that is slightly unleveled. If their surroundings are visually a mess, it can really hurt their brain. Yet, this is truly a gift. They can fix the visual errors like no one else can; things that could escape the notice of an auditory or kinesthetic.

Kinesthetics, comprising about 30% of the population, process information best through touch. Interestingly, they also have a heightened sense of smell, taste, and "gut" response. Comfort is a must in their lives, and they need to get their hands into any project they're working on or trying to learn. In terms of what's acceptable in society, kinesthetics have the hardest time. Hugs are extremely important for their brain, and, yet, we live in a society where proper touch is not validated. They're often shamed for their natural gift. If you fit into this category, change your mind. See your strength for what it is; a beautiful gift that should be treasured.

The third factor is Brain Gender. This is such a hotly debated subject, yet there's no denying the scientific evidence that the average male and average female brain is *structurally* different. This presents as personality strengths in both genders. For example, the corpus collosum. In most women, there are more fibers and they are larger in diameter; giving women the gift of moving with greater ease from one side of the brain to the other, creating the gift of multi-tasking. For men, this is a gift as well. They tend to stay in one side of the brain and keep focused, without being distracted.

Another brain gender difference is in the language centers. Men mostly use one center for speech; whereas, women can access multiple centers. In addition, the area in the brain that is connected to understanding language is 11% more dense with neurons in the average female. The results are that men speak approximately 12,000 words per day, but women can speak up to 50,000 words per day.

There are so many more interesting differences in the brain anatomy of men and women that we could write an entire book on them. But, for now, focus on the fact that, male or female, you have natural gifts connected to your brain gender. So, stop the criticism and learn to embrace them as the unique gifts that they are.

The forth factor is Brain Quadrant Dominance (BQD). To explain this fully, brain researcher, Dr. Richard Haier[9], explains it this way: "Most brains are believed to have an innate energy advantage in one of the four cerebral divisions. The brain uses less oxygen, glucose, and micro-nutrition, and needs a shorter recovery time when performing tasks that draw heavily on its area of energy advantage." Which of the four quadrants you spend the least energy in will directly affect your personality. The tasks preformed in each

---

[9] Professor Emeritus, Pediatrics School of Medicine PH.D., The Johns Hopkins University and University of California, Irvine

quadrant will come naturally to you, they're your gifts! I have briefly summarized them as follows:

You're the "Boss" BQD when your energy expenditure advantage is in the anterior (front) left portion of the brain. You'll be gifted in logical, inductive/deductive reasoning, making fact-based decisions and problem-solving easy for you. You're a take charge, delegate authority, type person. Debating and competition is fun for you, and you'll approach life with an objective, non-emotional view[10]. You'll prefer to be in control of everything. These traits are your gifts!

You're the "Master Coordinator" BQD when your energy expenditure advantage is in the posterior (back) left portion of your brain. This is where all the fact-based filing goes, making you skilled at recalling facts, details, and names. You'll enjoy and excel in sequencing and organizing every aspect of life. Structure is a must; everything having a purpose and a place. You're time conscious, and it's stressful if something causes you to be off schedule. For you, it's important to develop routines, and you'll follow them accurately - almost automatically. This is your gift!

You're the "Innovator" BQD when your energy expenditure advantage is in the anterior right section of your brain. You think out of the box easily, have a huge imagination, and enjoy daydreaming. You'll always be energized by innovation and brainstorming, finding the solution when all the facts aren't present. You love the big picture and are quickly bored by the details. The home of entrepreneurialism is housed in this section of the brain, so you're a true entrepreneur. These are your gifts!

You're the "Nurturer" BQD when your energy expenditure advantage is in the posterior right section of your brain. This is the

---

[10] The brain's right hemisphere has many more neural connections to the limbic center (the seat of emotions) than the left, so left-brainers typically display less emotion.

most emotional portion of the brain, making you gifted in showing, expressing, and feeling it. Your memory is based on emotions and feelings more than facts. You're dramatic, creating great acting ability. Peace and harmony are a must for you, and you'll avoid conflict as much as possible. The home of music is in this section of the brain; therefore, you have a natural musical ability. You love being with people and will seek out any and all opportunities to connect with others. These are your gifts!

Did you find your BQD? Were you able to identify what your brain personality profile might be? Well, hang on, because now I'm at the most complicated part of the brain personality connection - nurture.

Nurture

Nurture covers a wide range of external influences that can create a true internal struggle between who you are naturally and who you think you should be. When you're conceived, coded in your DNA is that beautiful brain personality connection, and your brain begins to take shape with its amazing energy expenditure gifts taking hold. Then something traumatic happens - you're born. Now, as you're welcomed into the world, external pressure begins to mount. Your birth order, family expectations, societal expectations, culture, etc., start putting you into a mold that may not be the one your brain is designed for.

While some find that they're able to live true to their brain, most find that they've been so strongly influenced by their nurture that they've lost who they naturally are. Here is where you can become your own worst enemy. You begin to measure yourself based on what you *think* you should be good at instead of seeing and embracing your natural gifts; never finding your power and then, with strength and pride, stepping into it. Instead, you find yourself trying hard to master what you're praised for and suppressing what you're shamed for. The result could be that you'll find yourself spending up to 100 times more brain energy - second-for-second. In the end, you're left exhausted, frustrated, and depressed; putting yourself in a very dangerous position.

Science again helps us to understand just how serious this situation is. The study of psychoneuroimmunology shows us that when a person is experiencing negative emotions it will literally reduce the effectiveness of their immune system. In cases of chronic negativity and stress, they'll actually start premature deterioration of their cells! This, in turn, can lead to an unhealthy, unhappy, and shorter life.

What's the answer? How can you use this information to make a difference in your life? How do you learn to *"Step Into Your Power?"* The answer: *"Change Your Mind!"*

Change Your Mind

By this point, you understand the importance of recognizing your natural gifts. But how do you make the needed changes? The steps are simple, although not easy at times. In the same way that you change your mind about dinner, you can control your thought process and change your mind about how you view your natural strengths, non-strengths, and who you are.

The first step is to know thyself. Clearly identify and become comfortable with your natural BPC. This will take some thought and meditation; remembering there is a *huge* difference between what you do well and what comes easy to your brain.

Think: are any of your natural traits ones that you were shamed for? Make a list. How do you feel about these traits? Do you see them as negative? It's essential that you "flip" the way you view them. Be sure that you re-label them as *gifts*! The terms you use will activate the brain in different ways, so it's important that you see them as positive - *always*.

Now, identify what you *think* is wrong with you. Ask yourself: what's the origin of my negative self-talk? I often say: the most damaging things to an individual's self-worth are the "insignificant" things uttered to them by "significant" people in their lives. Did it start with a relative, a teacher, a person in authority over you? If so, remember: *it was just their opinion and nothing more*! It has no bearing on the person you're able to become.

Next, and most importantly, you need to change the way you talk to yourself. It's estimated that a person can "say" in their own head up to 500 words per minute with possibly 60-85% of those words being negative. I always tell people: your brain listens to what your mind is saying, so be careful what you're telling it. Pay attention to how many of those words have a negative connotation. Write them down in a journal, then change them to positives. Continue this practice repeatedly, catching yourself every time you think or use words/phrases that are negative.

Finally, surround yourself with positive sayings, quotes, and pictures that promote positive feelings. When you do this, you'll almost automatically start thinking more positively, talking more positively, and associating with more positive people. The results will be - positive.

When you use this information to become more comfortable in your own skin, you'll be more self-confident and self-assured. You'll look at others differently, understanding that they have their own unique brain traits. Most of the time these traits are not bad, just different. Taking this view will improve all of your relationships.

When you "Change Your Mind!" in this way, you'll truly be happier. Then, as a natural course, you'll begin to be mentally and physically healthier. Your immune system will be more powerful. You'll start out each day with new energy. You'll feel the incredible feeling of owning who you truly are. So, get going. "Change Your Mind! - Step Into Your Power!"

To contact Julie:

info@yourbestmindonline.com

(800) 783-5877

www.brainladyspeaker.com

www.yourbestmindonline.com

Tom Kavanaugh, MA

Growing up in a lower, middle-class neighborhood in Brockton, Massachusetts, I struggled with school my whole life. Getting accepted into college was a huge accomplishment because it never occurred to me that I would be accepted because of my academic struggles.

During my third year of college the military draft decided I should become a member of the Armed Services, so I left college and enlisted in the US Marine Corps. It was in the Marines that I learned true resiliency, self-discipline and persistence.

After being honorably discharged from the Marines, I found employment which would lead me to successfully working in the auto industry for twenty-six years. What I enjoyed most about the auto industry was learning how to help people get what they wanted in a way that was mutually beneficial and rewarding.

As much as I enjoyed my work, I always felt like a Wounded Learner in everything I did. When I was introduced to the techniques of Neuro Linguistic Programming, my whole world changed. What I discovered were techniques that could help me overcome my learning challenges and the emotional baggage I was carrying around with me because of those challenges in my life. That discovery allowed me to transform the way I learned!

During this period of transformation, my true passion for helping others overcome their challenges with learning, trauma and life emerged, and would lead me to accelerated learning and personal change work. As a result, I've become a Master Trainer in Mind Mapping and The PhotoReading Whole Mind System as well as a Trainer in Neuro Linguistic Programming, Genius Code, Brain Gym and Abundance for Life!

The greatest discovery I've encountered was being able to help those exposed to trauma; and that discovery would lead me to create The R.E.L.E.A.S.E. Method™, a multi-faceted protocol to release the symptoms and effects of Post-Traumatic Stress for Veterans, First Responders and Trauma Survivors.

Please allow me to share the benefit of my experiences with you by contacting me when you're ready to make your Breakthrough to Freedom!

Breakthrough to Freedom

By Tom Kavanaugh, MA

As we begin our journey of discovery, I'll explain the details of what can create mental freedom so you can feel yourself letting go of what's holding you back from seeing true success.

The journey begins when I discovered how my world could change by following six steps which ultimately led me to become an accelerated learner. That's not a really big deal for most people; however, as someone who experienced severe head trauma during my formative years, and who qualified to be labeled "Dyslexic," my self-image was so poor that I became the class clown because I felt if I could distract everyone by my jokes and antics, then they wouldn't see the Wounded Learner behind the distraction. We didn't know I was a Wounded Learner, just that things didn't come easy for me to learn. When everyone else "got it" the first, or maybe the second time, it took me five to six times through anything to really understand what I was studying. Somehow, my brain built patched-together circuits that allowed me to understand new material, and that wasn't much fun.

So, here are a couple of reasons why my breakthrough to freedom can benefit your journey. During the last eight years I've gone from being a successful Dyslexic, Wounded Learner with Attention Deficit to losing it all, including all my money and assets, my relationship, and some of my friendships. It's not to say that no one offered to help or support me, because they did. The result is, though, that when you lose everything, other people can only help you so much; and, then, you have to do the rest yourself. That's what our time together is all about.

You might want to study this chapter because I've learned how to reorganize my life through a profoundly simple, brain-friendly technique called Mind Mapping. (The world's most radiant thinking and organizing tool for the brain!) That's Step 1; write it out.

Another truly amazing skill I learned on my journey is called The PhotoReading Whole Mind System. Essentially, I call it "speed reading on steroids," but it's really much more than that. The one thing you want to know is that it completely bypasses the conscious mind's filtering system which any Dyslexic will tell you is like running into a stop sign every time you try to consciously read anything! PhotoReading has allowed me to absorb the information from over 5,000 books since I began this journey of recovery. Learning how to learn has led me to become licensed to train PhotoReading, Neuro Linguistic Programming at both the Practitioner and Master Practitioner Level as well as the Genius Code and Brain Gym.

None of what I've just described is meant to impress you; but, rather, to impress upon you how available these skills and techniques are to get you back on the road to mental, emotional and financial freedom. That's more valuable than any amount of money that you and I can earn; and for our self-esteem, it's priceless! What I've discovered about me is that unless, or until, I was willing to work on my own self-worth, my own self-esteem, I couldn't begin to think about rebuilding my life, or attracting anyone who might want to become a part of my world! So, Step 2 is to get your goals established in the right way so you have a direction in life. As a matter of fact, once I got me to where I liked me, the whole world of possibilities began to unfold in front of my eyes.

Ultimately, the goal was to help others who had experienced trauma: Veterans, First Responders and Trauma Survivors. I was fortunate to create The R.E.L.E.A.S.E. Method, a process to successfully teach people who have experienced trauma to release their attachments to the effects of Post-Traumatic Stress. Please allow me to be very clear here; I'm not a medical professional, and I don't claim this as any kind of medical intervention. It's simply an alternative way of releasing attachment to the effects of having experienced trauma.

Let's look at what's really in this for you. When you're finished reading this chapter you'll know the six "secrets" I learned to move myself from being almost a million dollars in debt (lost very suddenly during the massive Ponzi scheme era), to becoming an accelerated learner without ever having to feel "stupid" again because everyone else "got it" when I couldn't; and to being well on my way to building a solid financial future with mental and emotional freedom I never thought was possible. Step #3 is to focus on a plan.

I'd like you to understand a couple of things which motivated me to seek a solution to my life's challenge. When I was eight years old, my mom took me down to our local frozen lake to learn ice skating. My coordination wasn't very good after a run-in with a tree which a few years earlier had left a long scar above my left eye. After my skates were all laced up, my mom and a couple of friends helped get me on the ice. Just as soon as they let me go, my skates slid out from underneath my body, and before there was even time to catch my fall the back of my head landed with a major "thud" on the ice. The only thing I could remember was the stars swirling around in my head when I woke up. That was the second major traumatic head injury in only four years, and what really stood out was that my ability to learn anything suddenly shifted.

Nothing was ever easy after that. That's when my feelings of being "stupid" took on a life of their own. School became a struggle. It was no longer the fun place I liked to go. Homework was something that never got done on time, and usually wasn't even close to being right. My grades became a dreaded event, and when tests were given, my world just became a living hell because I knew the results before even taking the test.

Along the way, during my junior high school years, one of the physical fights I was involved in resulted in a fractured jaw and a broken nose. That was my third major head trauma, and having broken my nose a couple of times before that playing sandlot football, I was now breathing with only one-half of my nose.

The feeling of frustration all through my school years led me to want to quit high school and go into the military. Fortunately, some teachers who really liked me, talked me into going to college. College! Well, I finally got into one, and needless to say, my feelings of self-worth didn't improve at all. By the time I was half-way through my third year with barely a C average in grades, the military draft came calling. So, I went down to my local recruiter and enlisted in the US Marine Corps. Little did I know that I would really learn how determined I was to actually succeed at something.

After graduating from Boot Camp at Parris Island, South Carolina, I headed for Southern California's Camp Pendleton where I worked for a year before being stationed in Okinawa, Japan. Upon my return to Southern California's Camp Pendleton, one of the first things I had to do was purchase transportation. It was during that experience that I first learned what real sales, the one-to-one kind, was all about. It all started with a cup of coffee the sales person offered me, and from there I was hooked.

Upon completion of active duty in the Marines, my first focus was to get a job. This is where the thinking of a Wounded Learner seemed to really take over my mind because I always thought people had to be really smart to become self-employed. I had the discipline to stay with something until it was accomplished; the Marines taught me how to do that. It was just the fact that I didn't really believe my intelligence was high enough to go into business for myself. What I discovered when I got the job as a delivery/salesperson for a local water company was that I was working really hard to make someone else a profit. And, the more I worked hard to improve my water route, the more they made. Of course, I made more money as well because I was starting to get the hang of being a sales person.

During my time there, my income began to rise with each and every achievement of being one of the successful delivery/sales people for the company.

Then suddenly, one day as I was reaching up to take one of the five-gallon bottles out of the rack on the side of the truck, my stomach muscles felt like they were moving in a completely different direction than normal. I had torn my stomach muscles apart and required immediate surgery to repair them. Once again, I was directed to a new career by a significant emotional event which was to become the core foundation for the work I do today.

In search of a new career, I remembered the interaction I had experienced with the car salesman several years earlier; and at that moment, I decided to look at a new career. Please remember, I chose this career for several reasons. One, I needed quick money because by now the family had grown to two children to support, and we had to move into a larger place. Again, not having finished college, my options appeared to be limited in my mind, and I didn't think there was that much to do to learn how to sell cars. Well, I have to tell you that if you want to do anything right, there is always a lot to learn! My career in the auto industry introduced me to some of the most sincere and professional sales people I've ever met in my life! These were the people who taught me how to win customers for life; mainly, by always making sure the exchange was a win/win scenario for all parties involved in the transaction. These are the people who taught me how to prospect for new business, how to follow up with potential clients (until they buy or die was our motto), and how to ensure their buying experience was the best they could hope for. (Buying a car is the fourth most significant emotional event for most people right behind getting married, having children and buying a house.) I also learned how to follow up with sold customers to receive repeat and referral business. Little did I know I was being groomed to become an entrepreneur through all the training I received in a career which spanned twenty-six years in the auto industry!

Having acquired quite a few rental properties during my time in the auto business, it was time to retire in 2006. However, just before I decided to retire, my boss hired a presenter to teach us how to sell cars using a technique called NLP (that's short for Neuro Linguistic Programming). We were doing very well in our dealership, and I told my boss as much. He said not to worry because he knew I would really like the training. So, in the first 30 minutes of the presentation, I was hooked. It was a whole new world of communication for me, and I began to see things I had never experienced before as we all listened with focused attention to this new "language of communication." Armed with this intro to NLP, I thought it would be great to learn this new technique, and maybe become a consultant by teaching it to others. In the midst of my training, I learned there were other techniques out there that could help me learn faster, better, and with improved comprehension! Step #4 is to get yourself educated.

After my retirement from the auto industry, NLP Training was next; and, then I flew to Wales, England to learn the subject of Mind

Mapping. Next on the list was Minneapolis, Minnesota, to learn training in a unique learning process called the PhotoReading Whole Mind System. Just the name made me feel as though it was something I definitely wanted to learn since I had been challenged my whole life as a Wounded Learner! (Later I would be privileged to be interviewed for the program NLP Mindfest, by Dr. Paul Scheele, the creator of the PhotoReading Whole Mind System on the subject of "Mending the Wounded Learner") During the training there, I was introduced to a process called Brain Gym, or Educational Kinesiology, which is teaching the brain how to learn by engaging both hemispheres to work together through the movements known as Brain Gyms. All of these accelerated learning techniques have brought me to a point of understanding where I now know there are no limitations to learning except those we place upon ourselves.

These techniques, and the processes included in them, became my way out of the deep hole of financial ruin, emotional challenges and intellectual starvation. All of this happened within a 90-day period of time when a friend of mine convinced me to invest in this business he had been receiving great returns with for a couple of years. Without all the details; essentially, I invested all of my retirement into the business, and in 90 days it was all gone. My money went into funding a highly-publicized Ponzi scheme.

It was at this point that I reinvented myself by going back to school and learning how all of these processes could benefit someone in my position. I knew there were others out there who were going through similar challenges with their jobs being eliminated and their retirement income portfolios withering away to almost nothing.

Step #5 is to follow a process. What came of this were two incredible release processes: the Executive Breakthrough Session and The R.E.L.E.A.S.E. Method. The Executive Breakthrough Session is designed for someone who is enjoying a level of success in their life, but seems to have a glass ceiling of limitations that prevents them from succeeding past a certain point of achievement. This process allows them to move beyond the confinement of their thinking to new heights of intellectual, emotional and financial freedom.

The R.E.L.E.A.S.E. Method is a process based upon accelerated learning which teaches an individual how to release their attachment to the effects of Post-Traumatic Stress as a result of participation in a war environment, during work as a First Responder, or an emotionally traumatic event.

All of these processes work by improving focus to create options and solutions to solving life's challenges. In my opinion, one of the keys to that is Step #6: Learn how to make informed decisions. When getting ready to make a decision, ask yourself these four questions:

What will happen if I do this?

What won't happen if I do this?

What will happen if I don't do this?

What won't happen if I don't do this?

If you've focused on the decision you have to make when asking these questions, it's been my experience the correct answer will reveal itself by the time you've finished asking the questions.

So, here's a recap of my six "secrets" to overcoming learning challenges and personal pitfalls that seem to enter our lives at one point or another:

1. Learn to write down what your challenge is. This makes it real and manageable.

2. Write your goals out in the S.M.A.R.T. goal process because it clarifies your thinking.

   The S.M.A.R.T. goal process defines how your goals can be created. The elements are:

   S = Simple and Specific

   M= Meaning and Measurable

   A= Achievable and "As If Now"

   R= Realistic and Reachable

   T= Timed and Towards what you want

3. Focus on a plan to work your way out of the challenge. I like to work my way backwards (something about being a Dyslexic taught me how to do this very successfully), because it helps me to see exactly what I need to have accomplished and when it needs to be completed. Then I can create steps to follow which ultimately become benchmarks, or sign posts, along the way of the journey to measure my progress.

4. Make it a point to educate yourself about learning how to learn better, faster and with deeper comprehension. Remember, knowledge is only powerful when properly utilized! I'd recommend learning the following techniques and processes for self-improvement:

   a. Mind Mapping

   b. PhotoReading Whole Mind System

   c. Neuro Linguistic Programming

      d. Genius Code

      e. Brain Gym

5. Establish a daily process, or routine, which

    a. Keeps you focused

    b. Moves you step-by-step towards reaching your goals

    c. Rewards your progress at each bench mark along the journey

    d. Recognize that reinventing yourself, or digging yourself out of a hole, is done through following a process every day.

6. Keep your mind focused on your goals by learning how to make decisions. In my opinion, learning how to make informed decisions is the single, most important skill you can learn to achieve success in life.

My initial "spark" in learning how to learn came when the salesman gave me that first cup of coffee as I purchased a car from him; that was the beginning of my journey.

That journey was made possible because I learned what it was like to really earn an accomplishment, because in order to graduate from boot camp, I not only had to work twice as hard as some of the other candidates in learning the new material, but I also had to work twice as hard at the physical portion of the training because I was breathing with only one side of my nose working properly. That's when focus and will power were really born in me.

What's really important to understand was how it all began when I slammed the back of my head against the ice as I fell when learning how to skate. It was in that moment that my life changed, and I had to learn resiliency as a matter of survival. You can, too.

What if you were to let go of all that is holding you back? Think about the possibilities; after all, they are endless.

Massive Success, Always,

Tom

To contact Tom:

Email: tom@newtrainingstrategies.com

Courses and Seminars available through: www.NewTrainingStrategies.com

Call: (805) 746-5648 or Skype: Tom_Kavanaugh

LinkedIn: https://www.linkedin.com/in/newtrainingstrategies/

Twitter: @Tom_Kavanaugh

Facebook: www.facebook.com/NewTrainingStrategies

Liana Nicolaou Ferrier

Liana Nicolaou Ferrier is a qualified life coach, author and speaker. She has her own practice working from home with clients around the world using Skype. Her passion is learning about human behaviors and loves helping her clients achieve their goals through effective communication and gently challenging their destructive beliefs. Liana has experience with people from different nationalities and cultures and appreciates people's diversity. She believes that there is a reason behind peoples' behaviors based on their knowledge, experiences, upbringing, culture and subculture. Her background is management of a Medical Center where she worked for 15 years all the while researching about personal development before deciding to become a full time life coach.

She speaks fluent Greek and English and loves to travel and socialize. She is a remarried divorcee and a devoted mother and wife who enjoys walking her dogs, dancing, meditating and gardening.

Living on the island of Cyprus in the Mediterranean, Liana enjoys nature and especially relaxing by the sea.

Story of An Immigrant Child

By Liana Nicolaou Ferrier

I was born in a small city in a small island in the Mediterranean. I was the eldest of two girls. My parents were poor in money but rich in dreams and ambitions. When I was born, they decided to move to another country to make their lives better and to offer their children a better life. Better than their own. They dared to make their dreams come true.

At the tender age of 1 month old, my parents left me. They moved far away, as far as Australia. Armored with just a suitcase of clothes and a financial debt that paid for their tickets, they set off to the unknown to realize their dreams. They were stranded in a foreign city, in a foreign country who spoke foreign words. The streets they walked the first night there were foreign and so were the people. They didn't have a clue where to go. Eventually a Greek family decided to accommodate them in their guest room at the back of their house. What a relief - someone spoke their language. Despite their fear and hunger, they were happy, they had somewhere to stay, and this was the beginning of their dream...

I was left at my grandmothers. "She is safe" my parents thought, and so I was. I was comfortable, well fed and loved. My beautiful single aunty became my mother. She fed me, bathed me, dressed me and loved me. I had everything I needed and I felt loved. I also had my grandmother's undivided love and attention. Being the first grandchild, I was doted on. I was a happy, secure baby.

Then the unexpected happened. I was put in a long metal tube that rose up in the air. I was so afraid that I hung onto my 'mother' the whole two day trip. She comforted me every way she could, she hugged me and told me that everything would be ok. But where are we and where are we going? The tube finally landed and I looked out the window. What is this? Where are we?

We were greeted by a couple that were unfamiliar to me. They had big smiles and warm eyes. They were so excited to see me and tried to snatch me off my 'mother.' Feeling petrified, I kept thinking I don't want to go with you, I don't know you, why are you taking me away? I was terrified, who were these strangers? Why is my 'mother' allowing them to take me from her? *Please* don't let them! My fear turned to exasperation, why are they doing this? I am sooo scared! Mama, please take me! To my horror, my 'mother' said, "Liana, I am not your mother, this woman is." What? No! Please!

It seemed like eternity for me back at the house. The foreign couple tried very hard to make me feel loved and welcome, I could see the pain in their eyes when I couldn't warm to them, but I just wanted my mama. I wanted to go home and see my grandma, play with my toys. Take me out of here! Through the couples persistence, I eventually started to warm to the woman. Women are familiar and safe and she was actually ok; she loved me and I could feel the love. But the man? Who is he? He says he is my father, but what is a father and what do they do? Little did I know that eventually this man would turn out to be my rock, my role model and my hero.

Days turned to weeks that turned to months. It was time for me to go to school. My father bought me a pretty school bag with a picture of a dog on it. I loved it, I love dogs. My mother dressed me in a pretty white lace dress, I was so excited. I looked up at the multicolored big building beaming with excited school kids running around in the playground. This looks like it's going to be fun. I waved my father goodbye and walked into the classroom. What are these people saying? I have no clue. The only adult in the class is walking towards me and speaking to me. I have no idea what she is saying. I am scared. I want to go home. Why are these kids so like me and yet I have no idea what they're talking about? *Get me out of here!* I resorted to tears. I was once again petrified.

As the days moved on I gradually started to learn English. I could even sing songs and play games with the other children. I even took ballet lessons and loved it. The ballet teacher was so happy with my midyear performance that she asked my parents if I could jump a class. "No" was the straight cut answer. They were too busy. They didn't have time to waste by driving me to the other side of the city, an hour's drive away. Their priority was to work hard. Just like any other immigrant. 'We came here to work hard in order for you to have a better life, a better one to what we had, we don't have time for this.' I was heartbroken. I loved my ballet, couldn't they understand that? No amount of begging or crying could make them change their mind. I received my 'Best Performer' award at the end of the year show with a heavy heart. I was proud and sad at the same time. I could understand my parents though, couldn't I? I had to. Just like I understood that my parents had no time to give my sister and me birthday parties, have friends over, go on outings, or visit friends. Just like I understood that I had to stay for long hours every day at their factory where they worked. Just like I understood that no matter how long and boring the hours were every day after school, I had to improvise what to do with my time until they finished work to drag us home tired and sleepy, only to be repeated the day after. I understood all right, I didn't have a choice.

"Liana, I have some news for you," my father said. I was only nine years old. "Our business is going very well but we are so homesick, we have decided to move back to Cyprus." Oh, great news! Wait, wasn't it? "You will have to move back on your own until we sell up, schools in Europe start in September so we don't want you to miss the start of your school year." What? Alone? *You're abandoning me again?* I don't want to go, but I have no choice, my parents have made their decision. I decide to do what I know best; be quiet and just accept without any questions asked. The day has come for me to go. My parents and my little sister drive me to the airport. My mother tries to hide her tears from me but I can see her crying. I can feel her pain. "Never mind," I convince myself, "it will only be for a few days and then I can be with my family again."

Back in Cyprus, I am happy to see my grandmother. She is also happy to have me back. I am spoiled once more. I am allowed to play outside in my grandmother's safe neighborhood and I have made loads of friends. My grandmother does her best to make me feel at home despite the aching loneliness I feel inside. She even makes me my favorite, homemade ravioli. I can still remember her knocking on my bedroom door every night as I cried myself to sleep, 'Please don't cry, come and eat, I have made you your favorite, ravioli.' I love ravioli, I eat loads of it to ease my hunger, the hunger that I am unaware that I have, hunger for a stable home environment where I don't feel the threat of being left or sent away. I miss my family and Australia. The same question keeps buzzing around in my head: *what have I done to make them send me away?*

Six months pass and my parents are struggling to sell so they cannot come and join me. They make the decision that I have to go back to Australia. I am over the moon with joy; I finally get to be with my family again. Tears of happiness roll down my cheeks as I reunite with my family at Tullamarine Airport. I hug my mother so tight that we both break down in sobs. I am so happy to be home! Back at home I chat with my sister in our bedroom until the early hours of the morning; I am so happy to be with my sister again, I missed those big blue eyes and curly hair! We have so much to catch up on! My mother gets annoyed and tells us to stop giggling as we are keeping her awake and she has to wake up early in the morning to go to work. Yes, again, I understand so I am quiet and decide that I had better go to sleep.

I am settled back into my daily routine, school, factory, factory, school. I am coming up to puberty, make up, fashion, latest music hits and… boys. I have to be careful though, nice Greek girls are not interested in boys as far as my parents are concerned! I cannot disappoint them; after all, they have given up so much and worked so hard to give me a better life. I have to do what I know best, be quiet.

Just when I thought that everything has finally reached a steady pace in my life, after four years, yet another change. My parents decide that after all, we are moving back to Cyprus. Not again! I bid farewell to our relatives and friends in Australia and move back to Cyprus. Yet again, I cry myself to sleep. I want to be back in Australia where my friends are, my life is, why are we back here again? Why can't I be like all the other children who have a consistent life? Seems like my life so far has been about many questions. I know what my parents would say; it's to give me a better life. And they are probably right. I went to the best private schools, lived in luxuries, spoke two languages fluently, expensive houses, cars, never went without, so why am I feeling so insecure inside? I had no one that I could count on but myself.

My life so far has taught me that the world is a lonely place and you cannot depend on anyone, not even the people who love you, for they too, will eventually leave you. You have to be tough and don't show emotions. You do as you are told, no questions asked. I was starving for a sense of consistency and security. I wanted to belong. I wanted my parents to be there for me *emotionally*. I felt a sense of emptiness and extreme loneliness. These deep seated feelings I carried with me for many years to come, completely unaware that they even existed.

At the age of sixteen, I met my first husband. He gave me the time, affection and attention that I was craving for all my life. It should have come as no surprise that at the age of nineteen I decided to marry him to give myself some form of stability that I was subconsciously craving for. What I didn't know at the time was that I had none of these attributes within me, how could I have given something I didn't have in order to have a successful marriage? How was I expected to make my marriage work when I didn't have the vital ingredients? I was blessed a couple of years later with my first baby, my son. Eighteen months later, I was so happy to give birth to my baby girl. Alas, my happiness only lasted a couple of days. Following the birth, I was in extreme pain and could not move my legs. I was pressured by my husband and family to go back to the doctor. I knew that something was very wrong, but I couldn't risk being away from my babies. One night when the pain got unbearable, I was carried into the doctor's surgery and was diagnosed with PSD. 'We don't know how long it will take for you to get better, if you ever do recover,' were the doctors dreaded words. I was devastated; I wanted to be home to look after my newborn. I wanted to be there for her and give her the security I didn't have as a child.

I fell into deep depression, the physical and mental pain were too much for me to bear. When released from the hospital, I was bed bound for another three months, all the time my baby in my bed with me, never leaving my side. I was very lucky that after three and a half months, I gradually started to get better until I could eventually start walking again. I felt so grateful and blessed to be able to have my legs back! Never in my life did I appreciate the great gift of being able to walk.

Unfortunately, these events started to take a toll on my marriage. Years started to roll by and I was just getting by. It wasn't a terrible marriage, we did well and built a lovely big house. I had two lovely children, we had our health and good jobs so what have I to complain about? And yet, something was missing, something wasn't right. Everything in my life seemed perfect on the surface, but I wasn't happy. I couldn't put my finger on it. I needed answers. That is when I started to turn my life around. I started to seek answers by examining my life and myself. I started seeing a psychotherapist, I wanted to find out more about myself and where my life was going. I started to meditate and read many self-help books looking for answers.

Gradually, the veil was starting to lift. My innermost feelings, thoughts and childhood pain were starting to surface. It was a long, bumpy ride, full of exhilarating experiences on the one hand and dejection and despair on the other. The more I got to learn about myself and life, the more I was thirsty to learn even more. I started to learn about self-love and my confidence and belief in myself grew. I wasn't that lonely insecure girl anymore and I didn't have to be quiet; I had a voice and could make my own choices in life. I decided that although my marriage wasn't 'bad' I wanted and deserved more. Despite the taboo and looks of disgust about divorce in my small community, I decided to leave my marriage. I wanted to go for *my* dreams and not live by anybody else's. Sure, it wasn't going to be easy, it was downright scary! The little girl inside me was feeling afraid again. She was going to venture out on her own, but I decided that I will be there for her every step of the way. I could comfort her when she got scared and tell her that everything would be ok.

I had a year to focus on myself. I had a year in which I feel I had the opportunity to truly grow. I felt the loneliness once again, but this time, I was in control. Now was the time to prove to myself how long I have come and practice what I have learned. I had to let the little girl inside me grow to be an independent and confident adult and I would still be there for her when she decided to come out and play. In that year, I learned more about myself than I had ever done. I had to feel the pain in order to come through it on the other side, a stronger person. I had to feel lonely and upset, in order to become responsible for myself. I had to, and wanted to, become my own woman. When I was ready to allow love to enter my life, I imagined exactly how it would be. I even wrote a list of all the things I was looking for and put it in the drawer beside my bed.

That's when I met my husband. We instantly hit it off and years later, when I found my list, to my amazement, he had all the attributes I listed! I had attracted him and all the experiences that come along with a new relationship into my life, and through him I am still growing every day. We support and challenge each other constantly and that helps us to continue to grow. He is the perfect partner that I have been looking for.

In 2010, my father lost his two year fight against cancer. Despite the doctors warning that he will only live for a month following diagnosis, he used all his determination to live for another two years. The man who was my role model, my rock, who taught me so much about life through our long talks, was now gone forever. The man whose passion and determination taught me how to be when you have a dream. The man who worked so hard in his life to reap the benefits of 'tomorrow' was now gone. As I held his hand until his last breath, the scared little girl inside me was out again. Once more, I comforted her and told her that everything would be ok and we would get through this together.

Through my father's death, I realized that all we have is today. Am I content in every area of my life today? Am I working in a job that fulfills me? I had to rethink about my career choices. Yes, I liked my job, but 'like' wasn't good enough anymore. I felt there was something bigger for me out there. With the support of my husband, I decided to take the next step and go for the job of my dreams. Despite my friends and family's loving 'advice,' I left a well-paid secure job. I needed the wow factor in my career as well. I had an urge to give to society and people what life had given to me. I decided to become a life coach and help other people find meaning in their lives.

I have learned that every so called 'disaster' in our lives is not really a disaster. Life throws things at us in order for us to learn and grow, and every experience shares a valuable lesson. Every pain serves us to gain in wisdom. I am now happier than I have ever been!

Dare to go for your dreams and don't let anything or anyone hold you back… not your past, present or the demons in your mind. Let go, feel free to express your needs, accept who you are and allow yourself the happiness you deserve.

Never settle for just ok, go for gold, live your life to its fullest!

I know that I will.

To contact Liana:

http://www.lianaslifecoaching.com

lianaferrier@hotmail.com

Tel: +357 257 101 45

Asha Mankowska

Asha Mankowska, Esq. is a Business & High Performance Coach/Consultant, Trainer, Marketing Expert, and International Motivational Speaker. She is a born entrepreneur, launching her first business at the age of 21 when she was in her second year of law school, successfully building three companies in Europe from the ground up and helping clients from several countries. She knows for a fact how difficult and frustrating any type of transition can be. Asha teaches clients from around the world how to achieve a healthy balance in their professional and personal lives. In addition to being recognized journalist, published in several European countries (mostly Poland, Germany and Sweden) and running very successful consulting and educational businesses, she has been an attorney and mediator for the past 11 years. Asha continues to be a successful and fulfilled Business, High Performance Coach & Marketing Consultant, Founder of "Speakers Bureau" for dynamic women entrepreneurs, the Radio Host: "Crush Fears with Asha" and host of video podcast: "Interviews with Asha: How to Grow Your Business."

In addition she is a Founder and creator of a business development training: "Hands-Free Marketing" training for coaches, consultants, experts, entrepreneurs and business owners. There are some fundamental things that every business should do if they want to prosper, market and make sales, regardless of their product or service. She has developed a marketing training program that addresses those fundamental concepts in 6 easy steps and teaches you how to promote and monetize on your business the smart way.

Manifest Your Greatness Today

By Asha Mankowska

"The foundation of our life is freedom to be, do and have whatever we desire. The perfect time to unlock our true power and rise above our circumstances is today." - Asha Mankowska

Most of us have goals and dreams, such as, to be happy, financially secure, thinner, or fulfilled in relationships; but all too often nothing is done to make it happen. We think of things or conditions that must change *before* we start, and set our sights on *someday*. "*Someday* I will lose weight, get married or start my family or business." Using this approach, 95% of people will never reach their goals.

My passion is to inspire those who have a deep desire to achieve their goals, those who are ready to make a commitment and take the necessary steps to turn their desires into reality. I want to inspire you to be in the upper 5% of the exclusive club of "Movers, Shakers and Action Takers;" to help you manifest your desires and your greatness beginning today. How many people do you have in your life that inspire and support your dreams and significance, and who can also provide you with the tools you need? Less than 5% of people have such support. I will give you the keys to unlock the powers that you already have in you, but which are for now, safely locked away. There are no conditions or special things to be done, obtained, or finished to start this journey - we simply start here and now. When you are ready to jump in with both feet, you will be amazed at what you can do.

Why Should You Thrive For Greatness?

Nowadays we have very comfortable and easy lives. With so many modern conveniences, we often don't strive for bigger goals. It is simply easier not to challenge ourselves. In fact, a culture has been created where we are happy with mediocrity, indolence and "no expectations." There are plenty of people content to live from pay check to pay check, and satisfied with the life of a couch potato. If that's a happy life for some, so be it. But that's not you. In fact, you could be a role model and an inspiration for others. My role is to ignite you to greatness, to lift you up and to activate your power to achieve. By power, I do not mean "potential."

Everyone talks about accessing potential, but for me, potential is like the Loch Ness Monster: everyone has heard of it but no one has seen it. It's very enigmatic and intangible. Potential is the capability to develop something in the future, having skills, qualities or abilities, which may or may not be developed.

Power already exists in every single person. It's a strength and influence that we can enforce and execute. We can make things happen when we have power.

A person, who unlocked their power, has access to their true creativity and freedom, lives according to their dreams, is motivated to be their best every day. Your power, the essence of your greatness, is this fire and passion in you, this magnetic confidence that radiates from within, attracting positive attention without intimidating or diminishing others. It is also the calling to be someone with a higher purpose; someone who has a desire to be the solution, not the problem; who seeks out responsibilities and challenges; someone reliable who can deliver on their promises; who makes a big impact and leaves a legacy.

Detect, Confront & Eliminate The Major Enemies To Your Greatness

"F.E.A.R. has two meanings: Forget Everything and Run or Face Everything And Rise. The choice is yours."

Greatness means reaching further into yourself and achieving your goals. In order to manifest greatness you have to be bold and courageous, shake things up and challenge the status quo.

Everyone talks about the perfect recipe for success. I am going to play devil's advocate, and talk about a perfect recipe for disaster. We all experience fear in life. Unfortunately, most people let fear, resistance, and frustration control their lives and stop them from achieving their dreams. They would rather stay in their toxic although cozy comfort zone, miserable, frustrated and feeling sorry for themselves, instead of taking the fear along for the ride and achieve whatever they want. It's incredible how people will do absolutely anything to avoid facing their fears. They will broadcast how much they want to achieve their dreams, and yet at the same time, nurture their resistance and all the "perfectly good" reasons why they can't achieve their ambitions. They run the risk of never getting what they want, and of being paralyzed by fear for the rest of their lives.

You need exactly the same amount of energy to stay in your status quo than it would take to remove the resistance and get what you really want. Just shift the direction. Fear creates resistance. Resistance is what our excuses are made of, and it is something that stops us from taking action and creates frustration and anger. These in turn create depression. Here are your steps towards failure:

1. Do not face and do not confront your fears.

2. Let fear draw you down into a life of resistance and inactivity.

3. Let this inactivity become frustration, unhappiness, and ultimately depression.

In fact, that is the perfect recipe for depression.

"Fear is not real. The only place that fear can exist is in our thoughts. It is a product of our imagination, causing us to fear things that may not ever exist. Danger is real but fear is a choice." - - Will Smith

Distinguish fear from danger. Fear serves no real purpose apart from hindering our actions and progress. They are just excuses to procrastinate and create a protection for own ego, so its feels safe and unchallenged. Fear seems to "help" by making us avoid difficult circumstances. We use fear as an emotional crutch for our weaknesses. We might be afraid of being rejected, isolated, abandoned, but those are only social circumstances that we can overcome. Take public speaking, in surveys it's usually rated as one of the highest fears, second only to death. Yet public speaking can be taught, learned, and mastered.

Fear rips us away from greatness. While fear can destroy you, the good news is that you can also destroy fear. You are much stronger, if you only allow yourself to be. You can either live the life of your dreams or the life of your fears. The choice will always be yours. If we can overcome our insecurities and fears, we can be successful in anything. The way to do it is to shift from fear to freedom, because freedom is the biggest motivation there is. We already have it within us to overcome fear. It's time to stop playing safe. You don't need permission, acceptance or perfect timing to be brave or see what you are made of.

> *"Our deepest fear is not that we are inadequate. Our deepest fear is that we are powerful beyond measure. It is our light, not our darkness that most frightens us."* -- Marianne Williamson

The Steps to Manifest Your Greatness

Your life does not have to be controlled by your fears. It can be full of strength, passion, financial freedom - you can live your own ideal scene.

While I can show you the way, it is your choice whether to explore this path or not. I am not introducing you to anything new that you need develop within yourself - I am only reminding you of whom you already are. You create your own life and experiences. You already have that power for inevitable success. Here is the recipe on how to access you greatness, and to manifest everything you want, right now.

> *"You can't solve a problem with the same level of thinking that created it." -* - Albert Einstein

In order to become the solid rock of your life, completely challenge your way of thinking. If you want to see more kindness, love, respect, and greatness, you have to become that person! I hope to inspire you to leave behind anything that holds you back, eliminate fear and resistance, and help you recognize, access, and reactivate your own personal power.

Step 1: Make a Full Commitment

"There's a difference between interest and commitment. When you are interested in doing something, you do it only when it's

convenient. When you are committed, you accept no excuses, only results!" You have to be fully dedicated, focused and committed to achieve your goals. What you are willing to do and how far you would go to get it?

Step 2: Ask The Powerful Question

In order to achieve anything, you need to tap into what motivates you the most. While people ask HOW, the most powerful question is: WHY? Your why is the motivation for your actions, especially when you feel tired, disappointed or overwhelmed. If your why is strong enough, the how is irrelevant. What's your WHY?

Step 3: Take Full Responsibility

Myth: We feel entitled to a life of happiness, an awesome career, nurturing relationships, and more.

Truth: There is only one person responsible for the quality of your life and only one person who holds the power to make it possible - YOU!

Accept full responsibility for your life, results, and circumstances, what you attract and experience.

> *"You are responsible for your life. If you are sitting around and waiting for someone to save you, to fix you, to even help you, you are wasting your time."* - Oprah Winfrey

Summon the courage within and change things around you. Take back the ownership and control: from victim to victor. As a victim you feel small, vulnerable, debilitated, stuck or trapped, like you can't move on. But whatever has happened in your life, take responsibility for it and for how you will act and react in the future, or you won't be able to achieve anything. When you blame others, you let them dictate your reality. Give up all excuses, blaming others, explaining why you can't or you haven't. Develop the identity of a victor, so even though you face the same circumstances, they will no longer disable you. Are you taking responsibility for your life today?

Step 4: Unleash Inspiration & Support System

Do you know why these 5%, the Movers, Shakers, and Action Takers are so successful? They have a dream team of supporters, mentors, and coaches. Create your own team that will make you unstoppable, remind you of your greatness, challenge and believe in you. Are you reaching out to someone on consistent basis? I will be delighted to assist you in actively pursuing your dreams.

Step 5: Become A Magnet To Attract Abundance

The principle is: *like attracts like.* You are your own gateway to prosperity. The *law of abundance* says that there is an overflowing quantity of everything in this universe for us: the health you desire, all the money you want, fulfilling career and love. All you have to do is unlock and receive your abundance.

It's your choice: do you choose abundance or do you not? On a conscious level, everyone chooses abundance and prosperity. However, on an unconscious level, you may be repelling abundance and be unaware of it. Being truly successful begins with a state of mind, with thinking BIG. What's your Big Picture Vision?

Step 6: Open Up For An Effortless Flow Of Prosperity

To be our own gateway to prosperity, we have to develop the concepts of appreciation, releasing control and going with the flow. As soon as we start treating life like as a gift, we open ourselves to an overflow of more gifts.

I was taught I must work hard to achieve anything. Struggle, effort, and hard work were always a part of my former mindset. But the more I studied the mindsets of successful people, I discovered how to *effortlessly* speed up my achievements. At first, it seemed like a foreign concept to me. For all lovers of hard work, don't worry, superior performance is still required. There is no magic wand that will allow you to just follow a successful plan consisted of quick steps to get happy or instant gratification. Success takes consistent effort, it doesn't happen overnight. The truth is that you can't just substitute "working smart" for "working hard" and constant dedication. You have to do both. But action doesn't contradict allowing; it's a key ingredient.

When we are receiving we are in a "state of allowing." Allowing means to deliberately choose your thoughts, words, and actions, to allow yourself to align with your desires. The state of allowing isn't a passive surrender to the universe, a state of inactivity and laziness. It's a state of inspired action, strategy and deliberate focus; a state of non-resistance that creates a momentum for the universe to act for you. You are the decision maker, you are telling the universe which direction you want your life to go. Allow the universe to play its role, provide the signs, people, opportunities, which will allow you to achieve what you desire. There is an ultimate balance between acting and receiving which creates *flow*. Going with the flow is a perfect way to accelerate our achievements. Do you know how to recognize WHEN to release control, let the universe work on your behalf, and receive?

Step 7: Manifesting Anything You Want

Everything is achievable. It depends on you showing up at your best in the world.

"When you want something, the entire universe conspires in helping you to achieve it." - Paulo Coelho

We are born with the ability to create a life of total fulfillment and the power to control our destiny. We do this by influencing our thoughts, emotions, and actions. Our thoughts and emotions create our reality. We can bring to us whatever we desire, because everything we think, feel and believe has energy. This way we attract and manifest a similar energy. If you are depressed, full of fear and resistance, guess what you attract into your life? When you believe in your own power and take responsibility for your own actions, you attract more wealth, health, and happiness.

Sometimes people believe they are too old to start something new, such as going back to school, getting married, starting a new business. Brian Tracy couldn't pass high school English, is now one of the top-selling authors in the world. Colonel Sanders, the founder of KFC, did not become wealthy until the age of 55.

What determines whether we live the life of our dreams is simply if we unlock our power. Once we envision it and *own* it, no matter what, we can manifest it.

Here are four steps:

Ask

First decide what you really want. Don't live someone else's dream - it will show by your lack of passion, dedication, and commitment. Instead, *reclaim your own power!* You deserve to have everything in your life exactly the way you want. Make a list of your dreams and turn them into a plan of S.M.A.R.T goals:

- Specific
- Measurable
- Achievable

- Relevant
- Time bound

It's like activating your inner GPS. Decide what you want and ask as if you expect to get it.

Believe

"Those who win are those who think they can." - - Richard Bach

You get what you expect, so believe in yourself and go for it. It's an attitude: failure is not an option. After deciding what you want, request it, and *believe* that it will be answered. Your belief must be so strong that you don't worry about *how* it will manifest. Just like after you input a destination into your car's GPS system, you don't worry about *how* you will get there.

Receive

This step is the most overlooked! The biggest enemy of receiving is resistance. How fast you manifest your desires depends on how deeply you believe you can achieve it, and how effortlessly you allow it to come into your life by removing resistance and creating space. As soon as you make room in your life, your desires will have space to appear. In order to get more of what you want, you simply need to get rid of what is no longer useful. Did you clean out your garage for your dream car, make time for new clients, or space for your soul mate in your life?

Action

"The distance between your dreams and your reality is called action."

Planning and strategizing, is great, but nothing will happen until you actually take action and implement. Most people spend their lives waiting for the perfect time and perfect conditions to start something. Studies prove successful people act, get results, and jump on opportunities. Unsuccessful people get the same ideas, have the same information, but they come up with excuses rather than taking action. Quit waiting around and get into the game now. Work your plan and never give up! We are being measured by our actions not intentions. What bold actions are you going to take today?

The Power of Now

"Things might come to those who wait, but only the things left by those who hustle." - - Abraham Lincoln

When we wait for things to happen, to be delivered to us on a silver platter, or depend on things outside of our own control to change, we diminish or surrender our own power. Summon and activate the courage you have within. Take back ownership and control of your life. Be accountable for who you are and what happens to you. You will then inspire others to be on the top successful 5% with us, initiating greater change.

We already hold the keys to our greatness inside. You have to find your unique way to activate and unlock it. This is the truest adventure you can have, and I would be honored to help you. Let's enjoy the journey! Success comes to those who don't settle for less!

To contact Asha:

Website: www.yourfavorite-lifecoach.com

Email: Asha_Mankowska@yahoo.com

Phone: (619) 471 6932

Facebook: https://www.facebook.com/pages/Asha-Mankowska-Your-Favorite-Transformational-Life-Coach/219849214774401

LinkedIn: https://www.linkedin.com/profile/view?id=173194011&trk=nav_responsive_tab_profile

Google+: https://plus.google.com/u/0/115390807162601572872/posts

Twitter: https://twitter.com/AshaMankowska

Anisa Hassan

Anisa Hassan is an award winning entrepreneur and author, based in Singapore. She's the owner of the international dating agency, It's Just Lunch Asia – an agency that helps busy, successful singles take charge of their love lives. Anisa has also been certified as a trainer and coach with the John Maxwell Team – a world renowned training company, since 2013. She has written two other books, *Guide to Dating in Asia*, as well as *Stressless Dating Solution*. As an Emotional Freedom Technique (EFT) practitioner, Anisa works tirelessly and passionately with women to manage their energy and equip them with tools to turn their pain to pleasure. She believes that every person has the ability to gain the most out of life when they first learn to love and accept themselves. Away from work, Anisa spends time creating memories and collecting air miles with her two daughters and husband.

From 7-11 to 7 Figures

How I Changed My Life by Practicing the Growth Principles

By Anisa Hassan

I have always been obsessed with growth.

At age 10, I distinctly remember sliding a ruler over my head and marking my height on the wooden wall of my house with a pencil. I would do it again every few months to check if I was experiencing any growth spurt.

Every increase in markings would make me ecstatic!

I was convinced that since I already stood at 1.53 meters (5ft) by the time I was 12, growing another 10 centimeters by the time I was 16 would be a cinch. Or so I thought.

But as fate would have it, the markings on the wall remained the same until the time I was 13. Not even half an inch more, not a quarter inch, nada!

In my teenage mind, my world had just collapsed. How could I go through life standing so short among my peers who towered over me? Their height advantage made me highly insecure and this vertical challenge could not have put a bigger dent on my self-esteem.

I experienced some kind of rage that life was unfair. I spent a long while angst-ridden through my teenage years, hoping that I could pop some pills that would make me grow taller.

My obsession began dwindling when I realized that my attempt to grow taller was futile. Who was I kidding? I was reaching the age when I would just stop growing. Even if there was a magic potion or a hidden insole that I could somehow purchase, I didn't have the means or the resources to get them!

When you grow up poor, you grow up fast.

At 15, my first job as a store assistant at a 7-11 store in *Jalan Kayu* shone a spotlight on my childishness. I didn't need to grow *taller*, I just needed to grow up!

My father was a lorry driver earning a meager monthly salary of $270 and he needed to support a family of ten! So I knew my education was on the line if I didn't earn enough money to pay for my GCE "O" level examination fees!

It dawned on me that I had spent countless days and nights trying to change *what is,* instead of focusing on what I could potentially become by equipping myself with the right tools and knowledge.

The issue with my height was no longer a big deal relative to how I could have a bigger, better life that's so different from what I had growing up! At that time, I intuitively knew that getting an education was my one-way ticket out of my poverty, and to get there, I needed the space to grow mentally.

Being given that insight early in my life made me resolve to go for what I wanted in life. It was as if something inexplicable had gotten a hold of me, and I became fully engaged in my studies that it made me unsinkable, unshakeable and unbreakable.

Getting out of my less than mediocre life - a life of hand me downs and second hand books - was a monumental driving force behind my almost compulsive behavior to succeed, at all costs.

Success in my studies came easily for me - getting to the Top 10% of my cohort was almost a given, but it came with the hunger to continually stretch myself to see what else was possible.

Securing a job before graduating and then being handpicked as one of the news presenters for a newly launched regional television station, were but a few feathers in my cap.

Yet, a small voice prompted me to look beyond what was easy and obvious and nudged me to explore the realm of what's possible.

It wasn't until I started my dating business - *It's Just Lunch* - in Singapore that I realized how much I had grown mentally, emotionally and spiritually. Growing my business from a one-woman show to a seven figure business in 3 years was what I have been preparing for all my life!

Remembering how much thrill and excitement I felt showing up for work at the 7-11 store right after school, almost 30 years ago, and having the same optimism and joy every time I head for work now, makes me feel incredibly fortunate to say that I'm living God's plan for me.

What I have also discovered is the power of growth within myself.

My initial obsession over my physical growth later evolved into a hunger for growth in life, leading me to craft my own Growth Principles which I believe can help just about anyone to grow in business and in life.

G – Guidance from God to ease the daily grind

Everyone goes through an awful period of being unsure, directionless, lost, confused, disoriented and vulnerable at the start of any new chapter or transition in our lives.

It could be a change in the school environment, the start of a new business, an upcoming nuptial, the birth of a child, the dreaded divorce and an inevitable death.

For most of us, to be dropped into such a wilderness and left with no guidance or no map, could easily plunge us into a state of panic. The thought of having to go through tough times alone can be very daunting for some, unbearable for others.

When the task gets too complicated and the responsibilities too heavy, there's no other way to turn but to God, who is truly in charge, truly powerful and truly in control.

I often have to deal with setbacks and disappointments in my business. There are days when I feel that I have worked long and hard to secure a certain deal, went the extra mile and jumped through rings of fire to prove that I have something valuable to offer.

Too often, things just didn't pan out the way I had envisioned or planned for. When I felt my patience running thin, especially when the results were not coming fast enough, I would turn over to God, to seek His guidance in easing my daily grind.

I would also play a game where I draw a straight line down a blank sheet of paper and on the left, the heading would read "MY Work" and the right would read "GOD's Work."

This exercise, created by *The Teachings of Abraham,* helps relieve me from the burden and feel less overwhelmed by the amount of work that I have to complete in a day.

Here is an example of the exercise:

MY WORK	GOD'S WORK
Recruit sales staff	Bring me the most competent, experienced and capable ones
	Make it easy and effortless for them to "get it" so that they can do their best work
Brainstorm with marketing dept.	Increase our brand visibility and help attract high paying clients
	Increase sales by 20% and profits by 10%
	Keep client retention and renewal at 30%
	Increase good energy and vibration in the office

To experience growth is to experience guidance from God. This means we will always be tested with challenges, risks, failures and a good dose of exasperating circumstances. But turning over to God has only brought peace, comfort and solutions that were never easy to see when I was in a state of panic and confusion.

I'm also reminded of a quote from Ramakrishna that says, "The more you advance toward God, the less He will give you worldly duties to perform..."

R – *Release yourself from victimhood, commit to taking responsibility and cultivate resiliency*

In my profession, I always come across clients who tell me that they are not able to find love because they are too old, too smart, too fat, too educated, too overqualified or just too unlucky.

Living in a state of "victimhood" robs us of our personal power. We can free ourselves from this painful and self-pitying state and reclaim our personal power by committing to personal responsibility and cultivating resiliency.

We are not born into a world that's free of judgment. When we step out from the safety and security of our homes, we will learn pretty quickly that not everyone will be our biggest fan! There will be people who will get us and there'll be others who just rub us the wrong way!

To experience growth, cultivating resiliency is paramount. When we experience situations when people irritate, mock, belittle, betray, criticize, condemn and complain, we can choose to take responsibility for the situation by assessing how we got into such a situation in the first place. Responsibility also means not meeting them at their level.

Some people may succumb to the interpretation, assumption and judgment of others, leaving them feeling defeated, disappointed and downright depressed. But others, who have cultivated resiliency, tend to recover better and faster from setbacks, adversities, illnesses and challenges.

Resilience means the ability to leap back and recoil. Just like in martial arts, the difference between a winner and a loser is that the winner gets up one more time. Similarly, in life, we are going to be knocked down several times with setbacks and downfalls that we don't expect.

Having resilience can measure how high we bounce back after a fall, because we certainly will have many falls that can leave us with scrapes and bruises but it doesn't have to be something that leaves us permanently paralyzed.

O – *Ownership of mind space*

Ralph Waldo Emerson once said, "You become what you think about all day long."

If stress thoughts are tipping the scale in your life, it wouldn't be long before you find yourself stuck in more overwhelming and stressful situations. If you're thinking of scarcity, anger or fear, then it's impossible that abundance, peace and calm will show up in your life.

Let's face it. Everyone encounters plenty of unpleasant, embarrassing and distressing situations. But I've noticed that successful and unsuccessful people deal with these situations in opposite ways.

Facebook postings are replete with examples of how the people who live with the invisible ceiling over their heads take every difficulty to heart. They dwell on the unpleasant instances and seem to be addicted to the feeling of being wronged and helpless.

Conversely, achievers "don't give another thought" to a situation that may have gone south. Like Gandhi, these achievers jealously guard their mind space and wouldn't allow the Mental Monster to walk through their minds with his dirty feet.

Now just imagine what kind of performance your car would deliver if every morning before you left for work, you scooped up a handful of dirt and put it into your fuel tank? Never mind its turbo engine, which would soon grind to a halt, unable to perform what it was engineered to do.

Similarly, waking up to negative and stressful thoughts produces needless wear and tear on our mental motor. It creates needless worry, anxiety, frustration and feelings of inadequacy.

How I've worked at keeping my mind space clear of clutter is to wake up with a huge smile on my face and immediately fill my mind with gratitude, for being given another day to do the work that I love and love the work that I do.

I have learned that when I start my mornings by reaching for the phone and checking my emails, my day went from 0 to 100 and continued to accelerate into a hot mess as I became irritated and bothered by all the impediments and daily distractions.

But when I turn my attention within, by nurturing and preparing my mind for a calm and productive day at work, no matter what the external circumstances are, I tended to wrap up my day feeling good and accomplished.

W – Widen your knowledge, environment and association with people who have blazed the trail before you

My thirst for knowledge is unquenchable. Sometimes it seems that I'm addicted to the pursuit and acquisition of knowledge, conditioned to take flights that could last more than 24 hours just so that I could be in the same room with the best minds in the world, attending seminars, workshops and conventions every year.

I vividly recall how I had to quickly find a masseuse to ease my twisted and "sprained" posterior from a flight that took me from

Singapore, to Moscow, to Houston and then to Chicago last year! But hey, I survived.

The legendary Jim Rohn once said, "earners are learners." He has also taught me to never begrudge the money I spend on my own education.

While accumulating material comforts came with fleeting pleasure, attending workshops and seminars have brought so much more value in my life. When I get to share stories and exchange ideas with people who are committed to their own growth, abundance and expansion, I thrive.

At the end of every event, I always get a buzz, thinking that, "If they can do it, so can I." Knowing that so many people have gone through the journey that I'm about to undertake would give me hope, optimism and a good support system that I can fall back on in times of trouble.

T - Take time to unwind, unplug and understand that everything's a process

We are living in a society of instant gratification. If there was a desirable outcome that we had wanted to achieve, we would have wanted it on our desk yesterday!

But "there's more to life than making it go faster," according to Gandhi. We are all conditioned to work hard to achieve all that we want out of life. That's why it is so easy to spend our life running on an endless treadmill, because we think it's going to bring us some place we want to go.

It isn't long before we begin to realize that we've been trapped into doing work that sucks the life and energy out of us. We find ourselves driving a vehicle that's running on empty, and the next gas station is nowhere in sight. We go through the rigmarole with no rest and no break and later discover that we find no joy in the process.

To grow, we can't assume that we can just go, go, go. We've got to have a plan, and we can't plan in a hurry! If Rome was not built in a day, what about the masterpiece of the life that we're intent on creating?

Taking the time to unwind, even if it means turning off the engine for some quiet time, is essential for our well-being. This body, the one vehicle that we have, can't be subjected to undue pressure and stress. Resting after a workout is important for recovery and essential for optimal performance.

Scheduling alone time away from the distractions and demands of work is an integral part of growth. It turns out that meaningful alone time is a primary need and a necessary tonic in today's rapid fire world.

H - Hire a coach to help you stay on course, eliminate distractions and build on your strengths

Hiring a coach is an affordable luxury that I now know I cannot do without.

Professional athletes and top business executives, who are committed to improving their strengths and performance, see the value of a hiring a coach. However, it is not common for regular folks to work with a life or business coach.

I used to think that I couldn't afford the cost of hiring a coach if it just meant keeping me accountable and staying on track. But I now see the costs of not hiring one.

My role is leading a team of women in my organization, and it is incumbent upon me to be the best role model for my team members.

Being an entrepreneur also means that I have to be the Chief Everything Officer. My journey is fraught with challenges that I'm sometimes the least prepared for, and having a coach gives me the comfort that I could turn to a confidant who can help untangle my raw nerves and deal with my problems objectively.

My coach, Marti Murphy, also helps me see my blind spots and nudges me to consider options that I'm resistant to trying if it had come from anyone else who didn't understand my level of hardship or my predicament so well.

As Albert Einstein posits, "We cannot solve our problems with the same level of thinking that created them." In the same way, having a coach gives me a fresh take on possible solutions that would have been impossible to see if I had only myself to rely on.

Getting a good coach is important because he/she can walk with you in your darkest hours, support you through your process and celebrate your success with you when you've made it to the other side.

My journey brings me to the conclusion that growth is an intimately personal matter. No one is there to give you a leg up, open doors for you and provide you with your lucky breaks if you first don't decide to personally grow yourself. Growth happens when you take the first step to fully own your life and decide what you want to do with it when you start seeing obstacles that you can solve or opportunities that you can take.

Growth also comes from within. The disparity that I see between the 'haves' and the 'have-nots' has fueled my fire to do better in life. Far from feeling resentful, I was grateful to be born into a large family where I had no choice but to learn to share. But the desire to break free from the constriction that my childhood life had presented to me propelled me to go for a life of plenty - a life that allows me to expand and have fun doing the things that I love.

Growth is also gradual and orderly, but uneven. When I planted the seed to excel academically, the outcome was almost always certain. But along the way, I had to put up with a lot of struggles and sacrifices that didn't feel like I was making much progress. Worse, there were times when I questioned if I was on the right path because the journey seemed long and arduous. But when I started my business and positioned it appropriately, the accolades and achievements seemed to flow so rapidly that I almost had a hard time catching up.

Finally, growth feels good. Just like a seed, I was in a place where I had to be covered with dirt, have fertilizers for food and not even be sure if I was ever going to make it out alive. Breaking out from my shell brought fear, discomfort and a whole lot of uncertainty, but once I started seeing the light and saw the possibility that I could one day become an oak tree, I knew that no matter where I was, I could grow as much as I wanted and reach for the stars if that's what I choose to do.

Now, who says I have a problem with my height?

To contact Asha:

https://anisahassan.com

www.itsjustlunchsingapore.com

Betty Russell

Betty Russell, BCC is a Dating & Relationship Specialist dedicated to providing singles with solid information, proven dating skills and an attraction plan to find the right partner. She is your guide to being a smart, savvy, effective, satisfied single while dating well and ultimately finding your true love.

Toxic Relationships - What Are They and What Can Be Done

By Betty Russell

David had been with Suzanne for so long that he forgot what it felt like to just feel good, or even okay, on a daily basis. He was in a toxic relationship but did not realize it. It was affecting his mental and emotional wellbeing. But he loved Suzanne - how could she be toxic? He had forgotten something: that healthy relationships make you feel essentially good - happy and energized. Sure, even good relationships have their ups and downs, but they are not *unhealthy*. Toxic relationships regularly make you feel drained, depressed and hopeless.

How do you know if you are in a toxic relationship or if you are just in a "rough patch" in an essentially healthy relationship? Stress, exhaustion, anxiety or worry, and other life factors can put a strain on even the best relationships. But a healthy relationship will rally because the partners in it will feel essentially supported, cared for, and validated. A truly toxic relationship will have one or more of the following characteristics *on a regular basis*:

You feel drained. You feel utterly sapped by the relationship, and rarely (or never) filled up by it, sustained by it, or nourished by it. Life can drain us - a hard day at work, a sick parent, a child in trouble. But when life gets us down, we want a relationship that can help us cope - not make things worse.

You feel bad about yourself. If interactions with your partner actually make you feel worse about yourself, not better - there is a problem. Is your partner overly critical or judgmental? Do you feel passively or actively belittled? These are signs of toxicity.

Everything is about your partner. Relationships with narcissists are almost always toxic. The fact that all roads - emotions, desires, expectations - lead to him or her, is a situation destined to be unsettling (at best) or toxic (at worst).

You can't be yourself. Do you feel like you can be yourself, warts and all? Can you be ridiculous, needy, angry, messy, compulsive - aka YOU - without fear? Or are you walking on eggshells most of the time because you are not sure what version of you will be acceptable?

The two of you don't share the same values. If you and your partner are working at cross purposes, things can get pretty uncomfortable. For example, if your desire for frugality clashes with his desire to "live in the moment" no matter the cost, and there is no compromise possible, this is a recipe for toxicity.

You disappoint one another. If you find you are constantly disappointed in your partner's behavior or comments, and can't shake the feeling that you are being let down on a regular basis, that is not a happy place to be. Or do you feel that your partner is disappointed in you? That no matter what you say or do, he or she feels dissatisfied or disillusioned... This recipe won't work for the long haul without some serious tweaks.

There is no safety. If you feel unsafe around your partner - red flag. And I don't just mean physically. Even if you know "he'd never lay a hand on you" or "she's never gotten violent," that doesn't mean you are safe. If you are fearful - of anything (outbursts, accusations, flying emotional shrapnel) - you are not safe.

There is no balanced give and take. Do you do all the heavy lifting? Are you always or most of the time the one to compromise, offer solutions, reach out with a nurturing hug, or back down from ugly arguments? Do you, in fact, do almost everything to make the relationship work, from cleaning the house to paying the bills? If your relationship is chronically imbalanced, chances are it is toxic.

You are overwhelmed. There are many situations that comprise toxicity in a relationship. If you feel the drama in your relationship is like a tidal wave and you have to expend all your energy just to stay upright, you are going to get worn out. The kinds of things that can create that feeling include constant criticism, demeaning or insulting commentary, demanding or controlling behavior, overwhelming negativity, chronic jealousy, or general emotional chaos.

Any relationship can be toxic - between friends, a parent and child, or co-workers, for example. It is rarely apparent in the early stages of a relationship that it will become unhealthy. In a romantic relationship, the positive chemicals that flood our systems in the first days or months, for example, keep us in denial even if we do see early signs. Whatever the reasons for two people to get stuck in a toxic spiral, things don't get seriously toxic until the relationship gets serious.

If you suspect you are in a toxic relationship but are afraid to talk about it with your partner... chances are you are in a toxic relationship. Fear of confrontation is a giant red flag. In a healthy relationship, you can talk about anything without fear of reprisal or judgment. If your friends or family have made observations about your relationship being unhealthy that you have vehemently denied, it may be that they are all clueless idiots, or it may be that *you are in denial.* Take a step back...

What can you do? Yes, you can change a toxic relationship. You can also end it - hard as that sounds, it can be done if change is not possible. You need to take action, as chronic exposure to the daily poison of an unhealthy relationship can make you physically ill. This needs to be taken seriously.

To change or end a toxic relationship requires self-reflection, inner work, healing, loving yourself more, setting firm boundaries, and speaking up for yourself.

Step one. Acknowledge it is a toxic relationship.

Seems simple, right? Well, not necessarily. From the inside of a relationship it is often difficult to recognize the signs. After all, you likely genuinely love this person. Your mind will not necessarily immediately assume he or she is bad for you. In fact - just the opposite. *You* will be more likely to blame yourself.

My client, Laila, was miserable and had been for months. Her partner, David, was her dream man in many ways. He was sexy, smart, ambitious, and playful. But too often, David was erratic in his behavior, critical of Laila, and likely to erupt into a rage at a moment's notice, especially if he had had one too many glasses of wine. Laila was sure she was doing something wrong to upset him. She confided to me, after they broke up, "I was sure that if I could figure out how to please him, we'd be the happiest couple in the world. I finally realized I was stuck in a toxic relationship. David seemed so perfect, until I realized he wasn't - at least not with me."

So if you take a long time to wise up to the sad truth, that your relationship is toxic, don't be hard on yourself. It happens. The more you try to please and appease your partner, the lower your self-esteem sinks and the more likely you are to assume you are to blame. It may also take a long time if you simply "recognize" a toxic relationship as familiar. If you have been in dysfunctional relationships in the past, it could be your "normal." So take a step back. If you are not feeling good inside - if you feel uneasy, anxious, or depressed about your relationship - look at my checklist, above, and see if you are, in fact, dealing with an unhealthy relationship.

Step two. Know that you deserve to be treated with respect, love, and consideration.

Easier said than done? I know that many people find it much easier to love and care for others than themselves. Even if you understand how important it is to value yourself, where do you start? Here is a simple guide for you to ponder - three aspects of self-care that you can meditate on and try to live, day by day. Whether you are in a toxic relationship or not, you deserve to honor, respect, and value yourself.

1. Honor yourself. Allan Lokos said, "You honor yourself by acting with dignity and composure." That means that you:

- *Live your truth*. It is your choice to align your *self* with your *actions*. It also means not sacrificing your best interests for the sake of others. Any relationship that requires that is not a healthy one anyway. *Embrace your authentic self*. What do you have to fear? How can your genuine self not be good enough? Any version of you based on what someone else wants or needs is not authentic. Honoring yourself means shedding false versions of you. *Acknowledge that your needs are legitimate*. Why? Because they are!

2. Respect yourself: *Know you are worthy*. When you realize you are not dependent on anyone else for validation or

sanction, you respect yourself. *Set and keep clear emotional and physical boundaries.* You would protect anyone you care about from being steam rolled, disrespected, or taken advantage of. So… that also goes for the most important person in your life: you. *Take responsibility for your own happiness.* Just as you can't be responsible for making someone else happy, or creating their reality, they cannot do that for you. Only you can. Once you realize this basic truth, you are liberated! Value yourself:

3. Live *according to your own values*. This means that whatever you display to the world lines up with what is inside you. And not only that, you have no fear of the judgment of others. Why would you? You value yourself and don't need anyone's approval. (You can see how this could be a game-changer in a toxic relationship.) *Realize success is what you say it is*. No one else has any meaningful criteria by which to judge you. What your mother, brother-in-law, boss, or romantic partner counts as success has no bearing on you. What you feel inside is what matters. *Appreciate all your life experiences.* In other words, value all the opportunities life has given you (the glorious, the good, the bad, and the awful) - for learning, growing, feeling, and discovering your authentic self. *Step three.* Work on changing the relationship.

Once you have decided that you are in a toxic relationship, and have begun to live according to the belief that *you deserve to be treated with respect, love, and consideration* (by yourself and your partner), you have a shot at changing the relationship. This change has to come from within, and clearly must be a value and goal for both of you.

This process involves four vitally important elements: boundaries, honesty, non-engagement, and (sometimes) separation.

1. Know and honor your boundaries.

A boundary is not a barrier. Fear creates barriers; self-respect creates boundaries. Setting boundaries raises your sense of self-worth and self-esteem, because you are sending the message (to yourself and others) that you are worthy of care. In a relationship, you want to respect and be respected, care and be cared for. Boundaries help make all that happen.

Boundaries can be internal or external, emotional or physical. Physical boundaries are all about your space, for example how much you want to be touched. In a toxic relationship, it is likely to be your emotional boundaries that are soft, and thus easily breached. Emotional boundaries are very important to your sense of self, your feelings of worth and safety. Important rule of thumb (and easier said than done): don't take things personally. What people say and how they behave is about them, not you.

The benefits of having healthy boundaries are many. For example, boundaries:

clarify how you want to be treated help you define your sense of who you are set limits on what you are willing to give (in terms of time, energy... even money) help you understand where you end and someone else begins protect you from having your physical and emotional limits violated In trying to work on your toxic relationship, it is important that you can speak openly about what is comfortable for you, what your limits are, and how you want to be treated.

2. Speak your truth.

Holding back is the worst thing you can do if you are engaging in a relationship detox. You do no favors to you or your partner if you withhold vital information about how you feel and what you want. Some guidelines:

> ✓ Speak about these important issues in person, not on the phone, via text, or over email. Make eye contact and maybe even initiate touch (hold hands, cuddle). Be kind. Use "I" statements. "I feel upset/inadequate when you criticize me, and I'm asking you to stop. Are you willing to do that?" or "Please don't talk to me in that way." Invite honesty in return. "How do you feel?" or "Tell me what it is like for you?"

3. *Be calm and don't engage.*

Not all toxic relationships are all about yelling and fighting. Some are more like cold wars, or feel like a passive-aggressive no-man's-land. But one thing is for sure, bickering, one-up-man-ship, or the classic "tennis match" of lobbed accusations and "but you always" serves, are all bound to have a most deleterious effect on your project of relationship detox. And besides: if you allow yourself to be caught up in an argument, you are giving away your power and energy. If your partner insists on a fight - say you are going to walk away. Then do it. Come back later and try again. Which brings us to our final step…

4. *Separate yourself from the toxic source.*

If you and your partner find you are unable to do any healing, because you always end up being triggered by the same old issues or beliefs, or because your pattern of fighting has become so entrenched you can't figure out another way of engaging, get space. By creating distance - i.e., temporarily moving out, limiting the times you see one another, or eliminating texts, emails, and phone calls in favor of only face-to-face encounters - it does not mean the relationship is doomed or over. Nor does it mean you are giving up on it. It means you are taking care of you while the relationship evolves to a better place - a safer place for both of you.

If step three does not work, move on to...

Step four. End the relationship.

If it comes to this, just remember a few things that may reassure you. Moving on from a relationship, especially one that is toxic, exhausts you, and leaves you feeling bad about yourself, is a chance to rediscover yourself, set new goals, reconnect with family and friends.

Whether you are able to change the relationship for the better, or you have to end it, it is important that you take time to process. Ask yourself, "What kept me in that relationship? What did I get out of it?" You may have felt comfortable because it was familiar, which means you could be repeating patterns from past relationships. Don't beat yourself up for that. It is very common and takes conscious work to break the cycle. Ask yourself what your attachment wounds are. Perhaps they are at the root of why you stuck it out as long as you did in a damaging relationship. Acknowledging those wounds, honoring them, and healing them will take some time, but it will be worth it to help you avoid attracting toxic relationships in the future.

If you stay in the relationship in order to heal it, seek counseling. Figure out together what brought you both to that toxic place. But if you end the relationship, don't spend a moment trying to figure out what made your partner tick. That is irrelevant at this point. Focus on you. Love yourself more. Forgive yourself for your contribution to the relationship. Do things for yourself that bring you peace.

In the end, try to feel some gratitude about what you learned, what you gained from the relationship, and for discovering what nourishes you and makes you happy - so you can go out and find it.

If you can trust yourself to set and keep boundaries, you will avoid toxicity in your life. Go forth and prosper in love - with health and happiness!

To contact Betty:

Claim your FREE "4 Steps To Find Your Future Love Fast!" visit www.BeFreeToLove.com Betty Russell, BCC

Dating Expert, Educator, Coach

www.BeFreeToLove.com

(615) 283-3393 Central

Skype: coach.bettyrussell

AFTERWORD

Life is always a series of transitions… people, places and things that shape who we are as individuals. Often, you never know that the next catalyst for change is around the corner.

Jim Britt and Jim Lutes have spent decades influencing individuals to blossom into the best version of themselves.

Allow all you have read in this book to create introspection and redirection if required. It's your journey to craft.

The Change is a series. A global movement. Watch for future releases and add them to your collection. If you know of anyone who would like to be considered as a co-author for a future book, have them email our offices at support@jimbritt.com.

The individual and combined works of Jim Britt and Jim Lutes have filled seminar rooms to maximum capacity and created a worldwide demand.

The blessings go both ways as Jim and Jim are always willing students of life. Out of demand for life changing programs and events, Jim and Jim conduct seminars worldwide as well as created a global company in over 170 countries called Quanta International, that allows anyone to benefit behaviorally as well as financially.

If you would like to hear more about how the Quanta company can assist you in both income generating and personal development, please email our offices at: quanta@jimbritt.com.

To Schedule Jim Britt or Jim Lutes as your featured speaker at your next convention or special event, email: support@jimbritt.com

Master your moment as they become hours that become days.

Your legacy awaits.

Blessings,

Jim Britt and Jim Lutes

www.ingramcontent.com/pod-product-compliance
Lightning Source LLC
Chambersburg PA
CBHW071900290426
44110CB00013B/1220